Sewing
with
Knits

Sewing
with
Knits

Classic, Stylish Garments
from Swimsuits
to Eveningwear

Connie Long

The Taunton Press

Cover photo: **Jack Deutsch**

Publisher: **Jim Childs**
Acquisitions Editor: **Jolynn Gower**
Assistant Editor: **Sarah Coe**
Copy Editor: **Diane Sinitsky**
Interior Designer: **Susan Fazekas**
Cover Designer, Layout Artist: **Lynne Phillips**
Illustrator: **Ron Carboni**
Indexer: **Lynda Stannard**
Photographers: **Jack Deutsch** (fashion shots), **Scott Phillips** (process shots)

Taunton
BOOKS & VIDEOS

for fellow enthusiasts

Text © 2000 by Connie Long
Photographs © 2000 by The Taunton Press, Inc.
Illustrations © 2000 by The Taunton Press, Inc.

Printed in the United States of America
10 9 8 7 6 5 4 3 2 1

The Taunton Press, Inc., 63 South Main Street, PO Box 5506, Newtown, CT 06470-5506
e-mail: tp@taunton.com

Distributed by Publishers Group West

Library of Congress Cataloging-in-Publication Data
    Long, Connie.
        Sewing with knits : classic, stylish garments : from swimsuits to eveningwear /
    Connie Long.
            p.   cm.
        ISBN 1-56158-311-1
        1. Sewing. 2. Knit goods I. Title.
    TT715.L66   2000
    646'.11—dc21   99–042160
                                                            CIP

To all who "build" things with fabric.
The endless combinations of colors, shapes, and
textures are full of possibilities that make the
process so rewarding and the results gratifying.

Contents

Introduction

There's much to like about sewing and wearing knits because they are easy to sew, comfortable to wear, and easy to care for. This book is dedicated to helping you sew a variety of knits successfully with the equipment you already own.

I am often asked if knits are easy or difficult to sew. My short answer is that they are just different. Here is my longer answer. The thing that makes all knits different from woven fabrics and all knits different from each other is the stretch. Because of the stretch, there are more variables to consider when sewing knitted fabrics, but stretch also makes knits more forgiving, especially when it comes to patterns. Patterns for knits are about simplicity. Knitted fabrics can mold to the body without complex tailoring. Easy patterns equal less time spent cutting, sewing, and fitting. I hope this last statement catches your attention because knitted garments are faster and easier to construct overall than woven garments.

You may be familiar with the basic knits, but there also are many specialty and exotic knits that reflect fashion trends and are interesting alternatives to their woven counterparts. When sheer fabrics are in style, you can expect to find sheer knits such as stretch illusion at fabric stores. Stretch velvets, laces, tweeds, sheers, lamé, sweaterknits, and synthetic fleece are just some of the many knit variations. These stretch versions of woven fabrics are exciting to see because the construction of knitted garments is always simpler than that of their woven counterparts. With the information in this book, you can sew any of these knits and get great results.

The first two chapters will help you get started. You will learn how knits are made and how they differ from wovens, and you'll find useful information for selecting a pattern, notions, and fabric. Chapters 3 and 4 contain essential techniques that work on a variety of knits. The methods you select will depend on your equipment, your skill, and your personal taste. Chapters 5 and 6 include sewing information that is specific to certain fabrics. Included throughout the book are decorative techniques because much of the fun in sewing has to do with playing and creating with fabric.

I hope this book will give you an understanding of sewing with all types of knits and the confidence to part with the printed pattern directions. Most of all, I hope this book will inspire you to take a basic pattern a step further to create beautiful, one-of-a-kind knit garments.

1 What Is a Knit?

It's hard to imagine a modern wardrobe that doesn't include some knitted garments. Knits are so comfortable to wear. They are used in all types of garments from the most sporty to the most practical to the most elegant. Knitted fabrics come in a variety of textures, fibers, weights, and colors. And best of all, knits are easy to sew once you learn what to expect from the various fabrics and how simple they are to construct.

Knitting is the second most common method of constructing cloth after weaving. Knitted textiles are made using needles and one or more yarns looped together to support one another, creating a porous and elastic fabric. Woven textiles, on the other hand, are created by interlacing two sets of yarns at right angles.

Sewing with knits has several advantages over wovens, and today you have a wide variety of knits from which to choose.

> **TIP**
>
> The type of yarn and the type of construction determine the amount of stretch in knitted fabric.

WHY SEW WITH KNITS?

One advantage of knitted fabrics is that they are flexible. This flexibility is an asset for the sewer since you can tailor the garment without having to struggle with the fit. Easy, simple shapes conform to the body because knitted fabrics mold nicely without needing precision tailoring.

Mainly because of the way knitted fabrics are constructed, all knits resist wrinkles better than their woven counterparts (even linen knits), making them easy to care for. Washable knits can go from the washer to the dryer to the wearer without needing any pressing. Both washable and dry-clean-only knits easily shed any wrinkling that might occur from wearing, so they are perfect for travel.

Comfort is the universal reason why everyone loves knits. That is why knits are so popular for sportswear, casuals, and loungewear, but you don't have to be at all sporty to love knits. The variety of knits is ever growing and you are sure to find a knitted fabric to fit every occasion.

TYPES OF KNITS

There are two basic types of machine-knitted fabrics: weft knits and warp knits. Weft is synonymous with filling in weaving and signifies crosswise looping in knitting. Weft knitting is like hand-knitting in that it uses the same basic stitches: plain, purl, and rib. Rows of loops, each caught into the previous row, create the fabric on a circular- or flat-knitting machine. Some examples of weft knitting are single knits, sweatshirt knits, double knits, interlocks, stretch velours, and sweaterbodies. Other variations include fabrics with openwork stitches, such as pointelles and knitted laces, as well as jacquard patterned knits. Weft knits typically have greater stretch than warp knits do.

Warp is synonymous with the length-wise direction in weaving. Warp knitting is done on a machine called a chain loom and can't be done by hand. Parallel yarns are arranged on the loom, then needles for each warp yarn form loops simultaneously in the lengthwise direction. The chains of parallel yarns are connected by the zigzag of the yarns from one needle to the other. Examples of warp knits are tricot and raschel knits. Raschel knits include a wide range of knits from fine-mesh to thick-pile fabrics. Fine warp knits such as tricot and some raschel knits can have a closer construction than weft-knitted fabrics.

HOW KNITS DIFFER FROM WOVENS

Knits differ from wovens in many ways. Because knitted fabrics conform to the body much more easily than woven fabrics, it is possible to simplify construction without sacrificing the shape. Darts become unnecessary, and zippers can be eliminated because even close-fitting knits fit over the body easily.

Knitted fabrics don't need as much ease as wovens. In fact, depending on the type of knit you are using and the amount of stretch it has, the garment can have zero ease or even negative ease. Swimsuits and leotards are examples of garments that are smaller than the body and have negative ease. They are also great examples of very close-fitting garments that can be sewn and worn without restricting movement or comfort.

It isn't always easy to tell whether a fabric is knit or woven, since the texture of the yarn and the complexity of the stitch can obscure the fabric's structure. If you want to find out which it is, unravel a crosswise yarn. A knit will have loops, while a woven fabric will fringe.

Knitted fabrics do not have selvages, and instead of a lengthwise and crosswise grain, they have lengthwise loops called wales and crosswise rows of loops called

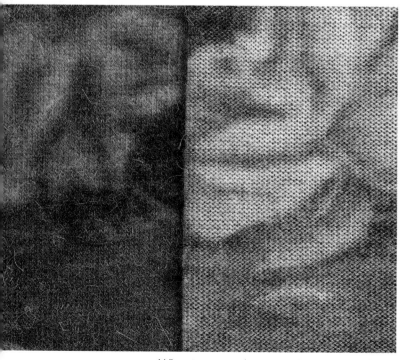

When you unravel a crosswise yarn, knitted fabric will have loops while a woven fabric will fringe.

courses. Just like woven fabrics, most knits have more stretch in one direction than another, but the amount of stretch varies greatly from one fabric to the next. Wovens have the greatest amount of stretch on the bias, while knits have the greatest amount of stretch crosswise. Some knits, such as swimsuit fabrics, have the greatest stretch lengthwise.

SELECTING FABRICS

These days, the selection of knits available to the home sewer is increasingly diverse, ranging from sheer gossamer knits such as stretch illusion, stretch chiffon, and mesh at the most lightweight end of the spectrum, all the way to thick, warm, and fluffy synthetic fleece and pile knits that resemble fur. Stretch laces, actionwear, and swimsuit fabrics keep getting more interesting; they contain lots of spandex and are functional as well as pretty. Novelty fabrics in this category may have shiny or matte finishes, textured surfaces, metallic yarns, or metallic prints.

Napped pile knits can be sporty, such as stretch terry, velour, or stretch suede cloth, or can look elegant and dressy, such as stretch velvet, stretch cut velvets, stretch panne velvet, stretch crushed velvet, and chenille. Sweaterknits may be plain jersey stitch in a basic cotton, warm lamb's wool, or luxurious cashmere. Other sweaterknits have novelty stitches or yarns or openwork stitches that resemble hand crochet. Stretch lamé, slinky knits, and matte jersey have the look and drape of silk wovens plus the comfort of a knitted fabric. With this huge range available, the home sewer can sew a complete wardrobe using knitted fabrics.

When choosing a fabric, color and texture are typically the first things to attract your attention, but base your fabric selection on the weight and thickness, drape, fiber content, and degree of stretch. Other factors to consider include care and maintenance, wrinkle resistance, and shape retention.

Base your fabric selection on the weight and thickness, drape, fiber content, and amount of stretch in the fabric. Care and maintenance and shape retention are other considerations.

The drape, or hand, of a knit is easy to determine by holding up the fabric and draping it on your body. This makes it easy to identify a fluid knit that drapes or a stable knit that holds its shape.

Knowing the fiber content can help you anticipate certain results from certain fibers. The amount of stretch in a fabric is determined by the fiber content and the stitch. If you take the same type of knit—jersey for example—and change the fiber content or how loosely or tightly knitted it is, then you change the amount of stretch and the amount of shrinkage in the final fabric.

Fabrics with different fiber contents have different characteristics. Cotton knits are comfortable to wear year-round and are available in a variety of weights and tex-

tures. Wool knits are elastic and retain their shape, while silk, rayon, linen, and ramie knits tend to be more droopy and have less recovery. All of these breathe well and are comfortable to wear. All knitted fabrics that contain some spandex have increased shape retention and elasticity.

Expect to dry-clean wool, silk, and rayon knits unless otherwise stated, or test-wash a sample of the fabric to see if you like the results. Knits made with synthetic fibers such as nylon, polyester, and acrylic are making a fashion comeback. These are easy to care for and dry easily but don't breathe well. The new microfiber knits we are starting to see should be more comfortable to wear, just like microfiber wovens.

There are numerous knit fabrics from which to choose, but they all fall into one of three general categories: basic knits; ribbed knits, sweaterknits, and openwork raschel knits; and fancy knits.

Basic Knits

Single knits, double knits, interlocks, and sweatshirt knits are the most readily available and recognizable weft knits on the market. These stable, basic knits have subtle differences and similarities. One similarity is that they all look the same on the right side, having flat, lengthwise ribs. The wrong side may have crosswise courses, look the same as the right side, or have a soft, brushed surface.

Single knits   Basic single knits, also called jersey, are plain-knit fabrics that have flat vertical ribs on the right side and horizontal courses on the wrong side. Patterned variations are created by alternating the arrangement of the basic stitches. Some simple variations include pointelle, openwork, and tuck stitches, but the pattern variations are endless.

Although single knits are most often lightweight, single-knit construction can also be used for a bulky sweater weight. Lightweight single knits such as jersey drape well and can be used to create soft or fluid silhouettes. Single knits, which are

Basic single knits, also called jersey, have flat, vertical ribs on the right side and horizontal courses on the wrong side. Interesting pattern variations are created by altering the arrangements of the basic stitches.

available in wool, cotton, polyester/cotton, silk, linen, and rayon, have less than 20% crosswise stretch and little lengthwise stretch. The cut edges curl to the right side and run from both ends, but they run more easily from the last row knitted. Knits made from slippery yarns, such as rayon or silk, run more easily than cotton or wool. By pulling along each cut crosswise edge of the fabric, you can tell if the fabric runs easily and which is the last row knitted. Single knits are suitable for dresses, tunics, tops, sportswear, sleepwear, and baby clothes.

Wool jersey is a drapey, stable single knit that is suitable for subdued evening sheaths, comfortable career clothing, and spunky casual styles with sportswear touches such as exposed zippers. You might expect wool knits to be fuzzy, fluffy, or thick, but they are smooth and tightly knitted with just enough elasticity to be comfortable and enough stability to be versatile. Wool jersey works well in patterns meant for woven fabrics and patterns that require a moderate amount of stretch. It is an excellent choice for pieced garments.

Double knits   For a double knit, two sets of needles are used to make a medium-weight to heavyweight fabric that is double the thickness of jersey. Plain double knits have a finely ribbed surface that looks the same on both sides, while fancier ones have a finely ribbed surface on the wrong side and a textured, patterned, or novelty stitch on the right side. All double knits hold their shape better than single knits. They are stable, easy to sew, resilient, and do not curl or unravel at the edges, making it possible to press seams open. Topstitching looks attractive on double knits and may be used on seams, necklines, edges, and hems. Most double knits have enough body to be used for tailored styles such as dresses, suits, jackets, and pants.

Interlocks   Knitted on an interlock machine, interlocks are made by interknitting two 1x1 rib fabrics to form one cloth. Interlocks have a smooth texture and look

Double the thickness of jersey, double knits are made by using two sets of needles. Plain double knits look the same on both sides, while fancier ones are patterned or textured on the right side and plain on the back.

the same on the right and wrong sides. These fabrics have more crosswise stretch than single knits or double knits and little lengthwise stretch. Because they are stable and will not curl at the edges, interlocks are easier to cut and sew than single knits. When using these fabrics, seams are best kept together because they will not stay in place when pressed or washed. Interlocks are suitable for T-shirts, sportswear, dresses, sleepwear, and children's and baby clothes.

Sweatshirt knits   Sweatshirt knits are bulky single knits with vertical ribs on the right side and a brushed, plushy wrong side. The brushed surface keeps you warm and helps absorb moisture. Sweatshirt knits are stable, easy to cut, and easy to sew. The use of this basic and practical fabric has

Tricot knits are fine warp knits that may be sheer or opaque and have a satinlike surface, a crepe surface, or a brushed flannel-like finish. Novelty and metallic yarns are used to create additional variations.

Ribbed knits are created by alternating the two basic stitches, resulting in a fabric that is very elastic in the crosswise direction. A 1x1 rib alternates one plain stitch with one purl stitch to create a subtle narrow ribbing. Increasing the number of alternating stitches makes the ribbing more prominent.

expanded from sweatshirts and sweatpants to other casual clothes, including skirts, dresses, cardigans, easy jackets, robes, and children's and baby clothes. Flatlocked seams are very compatible with sweatshirt knits, resulting in flat-butted seams that are also decorative.

Tricot Tricot knits are fine and tightly woven warp knits that are used for lingerie, dresses, loungewear, gloves, and linings. The name tricot comes from the French verb *tricoter*, meaning to knit. Tricot knits can be sheer or opaque and have a satin, crepe, or brushed surface. They can be made of single-, double-, or triple-warp construction. The difference in construction is not noticeable, but it affects the fabric's performance. For example, a single-warp tricot is not run-proof, while double- and triple-warp tricots are. Lightweight jersey and tricot look the same on the right side, both having fine-ribbed surfaces, but the wrong side of jersey has horizontal courses while the wrong side of tricot has herringbone courses.

Ribbed Knits, Sweaterknits, and Openwork Raschel Knits

Ribbed knits, sweaterknits, and some raschel knits have the homespun look of hand-knitted fabrics. The stitch formations include the basic and familiar rib stitch, bulky single knits, and jacquard patterns, as well as fancier varieties that look like hand-knitted stitches and hand-crocheted lace.

Ribbed knits Ribbed knits are easy to find in fabric stores. You can use them to finish or trim the neckline or edges on a variety of fabrics, but they require some special attention when used for the entire garment. Ribbed knits are identified by lengthwise wales on the right and wrong sides of the fabric.

The ribs are created by alternating the two basic knit stitches. Alternating two plain stitches with two purl stitches creates a 2x2 rib. The rib stitch can be varied by making the ribs wider or narrower. A 1x1 rib is very subtle, but more prominent wales in the fabric can be created by increasing the number of alternating stitches. Ribbed knits have much more crosswise stretch than basic knits and have very good recovery. These qualities make them an excellent choice for trimming other knits and for sewing body-conscious elastic garments without complicated construction.

Sweaterknits   Often bulkier than other knitted fabrics, sweaterknits are available by the yard or as sweaterbodies or sweater blanks. The fiber content, the stitch formations, and the yarn's texture and size all contribute to a fabric's character and good looks. The fiber content may be cotton, wool, silk, cashmere, lamb's wool, linen, acrylic, rayon, a blend of one or more of these yarns, or a blend with spandex, polyester, or nylon to increase the resilience. Expect to find bold and dramatic yarn variations, such as tweed, mohair, bouclé, Lurex metallic, nubby, flecked, space dyed,

and high twist, that add interesting texture or sheen to the knitted fabric.

The stitch formations and patterns on sweaterknits are just as diverse and interesting as other types of knits. They can include basic or fancy single knits and double knits, ribbed knits, simple or complex jacquard patterns, openwork pointelle stitches, and other novelty stitch variations.

Sweaterbodies   Sweaterbodies are knitted to specific lengths—typically just long enough from which to cut the manufacturer's desired style and as wide as the knitting machine—and have a finished lower edge. The lower edge is often an inch to several inches of ribbing stitch that changes to another stitch or pattern, such as a plain or novelty stitch, jacquard pattern, or stripe, for the rest of the body.

Sweaterbodies are a product of the domestic knitwear industry that is available to the home sewer through some fabric stores and mail-order sources. Most domestic sweaters are knitted this way. Instead of

Sweaterknits are bulkier than other knits and are available in interesting variations of fibers and stitch formations, including printed versions.

knitting the actual sweater shape, as in hand- and machine-knitted full-fashioned sweaters, manufacturers knit sweaterbodies. The advantage of using a sweaterbody is that you can cut whatever style or size you want from this basic cloth. You also have the advantage of having the ribbing already connected to the body.

Raschel knits Raschel knits are warp knits that are made on a raschel knitting machine. This versatile machine is used to create completely different types of knits, such as very lightweight mesh, lacy open-work designs, sweaterknits, and pile fabrics. Raschel sweaterknits are easy to identify by their parallel rows of chain stitches on the back of the fabric, interesting designs on the surface, and often a mélange of yarns. They can look bulky yet be loosely woven because the bulky yarns are used mostly to create the surface design.

Unlike weft sweaterknits, most raschel knits have little or no stretch and should be treated like wovens or very stable knits. A few raschel knits are four-way stretch fabrics and have maximum stretch. Raschel knits are appropriate for tops, skirts, dresses, jackets, and coats.

Sweaterbodies have a prefinished lower edge just like hand-knitted sweaters and are available in a variety of plain and novelty stitches and stripes.

Raschel knits are stable warp knits that have interesting surface designs and textures. These knits include lacy open-work and mesh fabrics, bulky tweeds, and furlike napped pile fabrics.

Swimsuit fabrics and other high-spandex fabrics are very elastic in both the lengthwise and cross-wise directions and retain their shape beautifully.

Fancy Knits

Fancy knits either serve a special purpose or add spice to your wardrobe. The variety of fancy knits is ever growing as new technology and new uses for old equipment result in exciting new fabrics and finishes.

Swimsuit fabric and stretch lace

Knitted fabrics with two-way and four-way stretch have the greatest amount of lengthwise and crosswise stretch and have excellent shape retention. These knits allow you to sew close-fitting garments that are comfortable, hold their shape, and let you move without restriction. Typically used for swimwear, leotards, active sportswear, and leggings, you can also use these very elastic fabrics to sew T-shirts, dresses, and other wardrobe basics.

Stretch velvet, velour, and stretch suede cloth

Stretch velvet, velour, and stretch suede cloth have a brushed, napped pile on their right sides and smooth lengthwise ribs on their wrong sides. There are just as many stretch velvets as there are woven velvets. The interesting and varied surface variations include panne velvet, which has a flat, silky, satinlike surface; crushed velvet, which has a shiny and matte mottled surface; and cut velvet, which has floral, geometric, or curvilinear sculpted surface motifs.

Basic stretch velvets and stretch velours have the same smooth and even velvet surface, but the surface quality varies depending on the fiber. Velour has a more casual look than velvet due to a higher cotton content in the napped surface, or pile. Stretch velvets are drapey and slinky, yet they are resilient and not as easily damaged as their woven counterparts. These luminous fabrics are typically washable. Once you sew with stretch velvets, you may never want to sew with wovens again unless you want to sew a structured style.

Stretch napped pile fabrics such as stretch velvet, stretch suede cloth, and velour have luxurious finishes but are easy to maintain.

Stretch suedes have a flatter pile than stretch velvets but behave similarly when you cut and sew them. Use stretch velvet, velour, and suede cloth to sew T-shirts, dresses, tunics, skirts, pants, leggings, shirts, cardigans, jackets, robes, or a dressed-up but comfortable version of any of your favorite wardrobe basics.

Chenille   Knitted chenille uses fuzzy caterpillar-like yarns often in combination with fine, plain yarns to create a plushy, napped surface that looks luxurious and feels soft and velvety. Knitted chenilles are bulky, loosely knitted, and sweaterlike. Most chenille fabrics are warp knits because warp construction keeps the chenille yarn on the surface and uses a finer yarn on the

wrong side, resulting in a less bulky fabric than would be possible using weft knitting. Because they are warp knits, chenilles are stable and therefore easy to cut. Most chenille yarns are large, which results in weighty, drapey fabrics that are appropriate for tops, tunics, and unstructured jacket or cardigan shapes. Pants and skirts should only be considered if you find a fine-gauge version of the fabric.

Terry   Stretch terry and French terry have loops on their right sides and smooth vertical ribs on their wrong sides. French terry has subtler loops and is more stable than stretch terry. In spite of their textures, both fabrics are easy to sew and are very stable compared with other napped fabrics.

Chenille knits are made using soft, caterpillar-like chenille yarns in combination with a smooth, plain, lightweight yarn that is more noticeable on the wrong side of the fabric than on the right. The resulting fabrics look velvety and sweaterlike.

Stretch terry has loops on the right side and a smooth vertical rib on the wrong side. Variations include French terry, which has subtler loops and is a bit more stable than other stretch terry, and brushed terry, which has a soft, lamblike surface.

Stretch terry is also available in a brushed version that has a soft, lamblike surface texture created by brushing the terry loops into soft, fluffy tufts. Occasionally you can find double-faced terry fabrics that are reversible, having loops on one side and a smooth, finished second side. Stretch terries are bulky, have variable amounts of stretch, and typically curl at the edges. Looped fabrics are perfect for robes, T-shirts, sportswear, and children's and baby clothes.

Synthetic fleece and pile
Synthetic fleece has a high-loft finish that is created by napping and shearing the surface of the knitted fabric on one or both sides. First

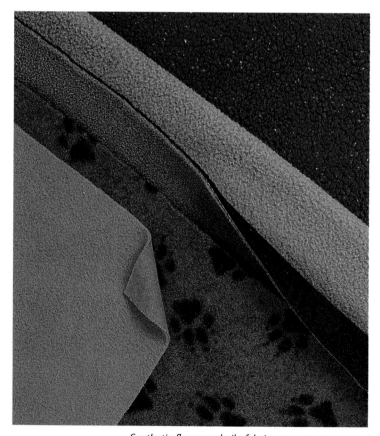

Synthetic fleece and pile fabrics are easy to care for, soft, fluffy, and keep you warm and dry. Fleece is available in many thicknesses and finishes that range from thin and lightweight to thick, fur-like cut-pile versions.

the fabric is brushed or roughed up to raise the nap, then the surface nap is cut to a specific length on a shearing machine, resulting in an even, velvety surface. Printed designs have soft, blurry edges because the printing is done before napping the fabric.

Synthetic fleece is lightweight yet warm and keeps you dry and comfortable because it wicks moisture away from your body, breathes, and dries quickly when wet. As the popularity of this napped fabric has increased, so have the varieties, weights, and textures that are available both as ready-made clothing and as fabric in sewing stores. You will find lightweight, medium-weight, and heavyweight fleece, but don't expect any fleece to actually be heavy because in this case heavy means warmer and thicker.

Double-face fleece, the most popular and easily identifiable variety, is napped on both sides. Single-face fleece is napped on one side and jersey on the other. Other variations are created by bonding fleece to different fabrics, by bonding two single-faced fleeces together, or by adding spandex. Everyone loves the feel of the soft, cuddly surface, which probably explains why its use has gone far beyond active sportswear and into casual clothes, accessories, and loungewear. The range of fabrics is so great that lightweight fleeces are light enough for T-shirts, while the warmer versions will take you hiking or mountain climbing.

Pile knits have the same desirable qualities as fleece although they are constructed in a completely different way. These are knitted with separate yarns for the base fabric and the pile to produce pile on one or both sides of the fabric. Because the pile fibers are different from the base cloth, pile can be made using a variety of fibers having different textures. As opposed to being printed, patterned designs are made on jacquard knitting machines. Pile fleeces are used for the same types of garments as synthetic fleece.

Slinky knits The first thing you notice about slinky knits is how luminous and interesting the surface is and how rich the colors look. Slinky knits are acetate and spandex fabrics that are washable and wrinkle resistant. Although the name Slinky knit has been trademarked by Horizon Fabrics, it is also used to describe similar fabrics made by other mills.

These are fine-ribbed knits that have lots of stretch and good recovery because of the ribbing and spandex. The fine ribbing in most of these fabrics is textured to look mottled or distressed, greatly adding to the depth of color. Slinky knits sometimes look sueded because of the way the light hits the surface of the cloth. Due to the popularity of slinky fabrics, there are many variations such as prints, embossed surfaces, flocked (velvet) designs, and cracked ice or glitter. Slinky knits are appropriate for tops, shirts, pants, and dresses in close-fitting or flowing styles with ample ease.

Slinky knits are springy, lively knits that have excellent drape, bounce, and elasticity. The textured surface of basic slinky knits adds to the depth and richness of the colors. Other varieties are printed, embossed, flocked, or sprinkled with cracked ice.

Matte jersey Matte jersey is an elegant knitted fabric with a matte, or nonshiny, surface that is favored by designers. It has a wide range of uses from simple but elegant T-shirts to cocktail and evening dresses for the dressiest occasions. Most matte jerseys are rayon or polyester, but you can occasionally find silk matte jersey. Rayon matte jersey, despite being thin, is actually heavy, which adds to its fluidity and drape. These fabrics have moderate crosswise stretch and almost no lengthwise stretch unless there is spandex added.

The majority of the matte jersey fabrics on the market do not curl at the edges because they are actually either very finely ribbed knits or very fine interlock knits, instead of jersey as the name implies. Wonderful to wear, matte jerseys are perfect for sewing fluid dresses, tops, tunics, skirts, pants, and separates.

Matte jerseys have a heavy, silklike drape and a matte finish. Most matte jerseys are rayon, but polyester and silk versions are also available. Other variations may have a distinctive crepe texture or added sparkle derived from the addition of a fine Lurex yarn.

2

Preparing to Sew

When selecting patterns, interfacing, and notions for knitted fabrics, the stretch factor must be considered. The right interfacing and notions help you accomplish the desired results and make each task easier. Special-purpose needles, threads, and elastics maximize the results. Before laying out and cutting your fabric, be sure to prepare it first by preshrinking it.

SELECTING A PATTERN

When looking for a pattern, you have several options. You can select a pattern meant for knits, convert a pattern meant for wovens, or copy something you have purchased and would love to reproduce.

Patterns for Knits

Patterns designed for knits take into consideration the amount of stretch in the fabric and therefore have less ease than patterns meant for woven fabrics. Because knits vary, knit patterns are gauged for differing amounts of stretch. The stretch gauge on the back of the pattern envelope will help you select the knit with the right amount of stretch for your project.

Patterns designed specifically for use with knits take the fabric's stretch into consideration.

Some patterns require fabrics with both crosswise and lengthwise stretch. Swimsuits and leotards always need two-way stretch fabrics, while any close-fitting pattern that pulls over the body without using a zipper closure may also require it. To be sure you're choosing the right fabric, compare both its crosswise and lengthwise stretch to the gauge. Fabric for patterns requiring

two-way stretch must stretch 2 in. or more for every 4 in. of fabric in both directions.

An advantage to using patterns meant for knits is that the styles and general instructions take into account the degree of stretch in the fabric. Pattern companies that specialize in knits, such as Kwik Sew and Stretch and Sew, have the best techni-cal directions, and the pattern selection is sure to include the types of styles that you would expect to sew from knitted fabrics. The other major pattern companies have more variety in styles, but their directions are less reliable. Expect designer patterns to have the most interesting styles and the least appropriate techniques.

Unless the fabric requirements for the pattern you are using are limited to just one type of fabric, you should consider the pattern instructions as general guidelines for sewing knits and a good starting point. The remaining chapters in this book include lots of techniques, additional information,

TWO-, FOUR-WAY STRETCH

Two-way and four-way stretch knits are fabrics with both lengthwise and crosswise stretch that look the same at first glance. The difference is in the amount of stretch and the thickness of the fabric. Two-way stretch knits get their lengthwise stretch from the use of span-dex fiber. Four-way stretch knits are heavier, have more body, and have more stretch because their lengthwise stretch comes from the structure of the knit in addition to the spandex fiber. ■

TIP
How well a fabric recovers to its original size after stretching is a good indicator of how a fabric will retain its shape when you wear it.

USING A STRETCH GAUGE

To compare the amount of stretch in a fabric to a stretch gauge, fold the knit crosswise a minimum of 6 in. from the cut edge, then position the fold next to the stretch gauge. Never com-pare the amount of stretch along the cut edge because it is inaccu-rate. To have the correct amount of stretch, the amount of fabric that is between the first two lines on the left side of the gauge must be able to stretch to the end mark on the right end of the stretch gauge (see the photo at right). Pattern companies typical-ly use a 4-in. guide to determine the amount of stretch in a fabric.

Stable knits stretch approxi-mately ½ in. for every 4 in. of fabric, or less than 15%. Moder-

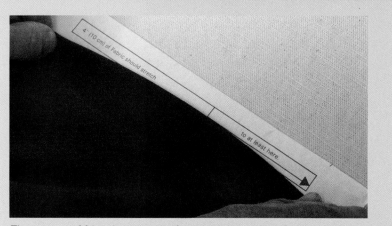

The amount of fabric between the first two lines on the left side of the gauge should be able to stretch to the far right end of the gauge.

ate stretch knits stretch 1 in. to 1½ in., or between 25% and 30%, and very stretchy knits stretch 2 in. or more, or 50% or more. Expect the amount of stretch on some ribbing and fabrics with spandex to exceed 100%. ■

and hints for sewing a variety of specific knits successfully.

Using a Pattern Meant for Wovens

Patterns meant for woven fabrics also may be used for knitted fabrics, but some changes may be necessary. For example, if the pattern is oversized, you may need to use a smaller size because stretch fabrics have built-in ease. Unstructured styles are the best choice, since knits do not need darts or extra seams to add shape. Other changes for adapting a woven pattern to knitted fabrics include changing the type of seams and seam finishes, eliminating facings or changing facings to bindings, and eliminating zippers when possible.

Stable knits, such as jersey, double knits, and raschel knits, are easy to use with patterns meant for wovens. You don't need to make changes to the way you finish edges or need to use a smaller size. Knits with two-way or four-way stretch, on the other hand, do not easily cross over for use with woven patterns.

Patterns with simple, clean lines work well in a variety of fabrics. When you are considering using a pattern meant for woven fabrics, look at the style lines and ask yourself if they are simple enough to use with a stretchy fabric. Look over the sewing directions. If the style has facings, is it possible to use facings with the knit you are using, or will the facings be too thick or too

These patterns can all be converted for use with knits with only simple changes.

THE BEST SEAM ALLOWANCE FOR YOUR KNIT

The right seam allowance will actually make your sewing faster and easier, so when you cut a garment it makes sense to change the pattern seam allowances to be compatible with the knitted fabric you are sewing. Pattern companies specializing in knits use ¼-in. seam allowances, while the major pattern companies use ⅝-in. seam allowances for all fabrics. Choose the best seam allowance for each fabric based on how stable the fabric edges are and how you plan to sew the seams.

Here are some things to keep in mind when deciding on the best seam allowance for your knit:

- A ½-in. or ⅝-in. seam allowance is best if a fabric unravels easily, is loosely knitted, stretches out easily, has a textured or raised nap such as velour or chenille, or slips and slides under the presser foot.
- Use a ½-in. or ⅝-in. seam allowance if a fabric curls easily. It is difficult to sew fabrics that curl using a ¼-in. seam allowance—even on a serger—because they have a tendency to curl near the edge and in the line of stitching. Sewing farther from the edge eliminates this situation. On a serger, allow the fabric to curl over the edge of the sewing surface so that it is cut away by the serger knife.
- Use a ½-in. or ⅝-in. seam allowance when you use a walking foot. A ¼-in. seam allowance is not compatible with a walking foot because there is not enough contact with the fabric.
- Use ½-in. or ⅝-in. seam allowance if you plan to sew seams on a serger. Trimming as you sew results in a neat edge. (I make an exception when using a swimsuit pattern with ¼-in. seam allowances because swimsuit fabrics are stable enough to serge near the edge.)
- Fabrics with stable, neat edges, such as swimsuit fabric, interlock, and synthetic fleece, sew nicely using ¼-in. or ⅝-in. seam allowances. If you plan to sew a garment using one of the overlock stitches on your sewing machine, it is best to use a ¼-in. seam allowance so you can place the stitch along the edge without having to trim the seam first. ■

structured for the knitted fabric? Can the facings be converted to bindings, or can ribbed trim be used instead? Look at the hem finishes and seam finishes and see if they can easily be changed.

You should be aware that styles that require crisp edges won't work or look as expected, since knitted fabrics don't take a crease and have an overall soft effect. A pattern you've already used and like is an excellent candidate for conversion.

Copying a T-shirt or Sweater

Cloning your favorite T-shirt or sweater is easy to do. When I buy the perfect knit top or sweater, I copy it so that I can reproduce it in a variety of colors that fit my wardrobe. Copying knit garments is easy—knits have simple shapes that lie flat and are easily outlined with a marker.

I use crisp brown paper to create the pattern, then I draw the outline of the paper pattern onto the knitted fabric and remove the pattern to cut the fabric. The stiff paper allows me to use weights or just a few pins to hold the pattern in place on top of the fabric.

1. To copy a T-shirt, select a piece of pattern paper that is large enough to outline the entire front or the entire back, then fold the paper in half lengthwise.
2. Place the center of the T-shirt along the center fold of the pattern paper and outline half of the T-shirt. To copy the armhole, either lift the sleeve and outline the armscye or run a spoked tracing wheel along the armscye (see the top left photo on the facing page).
3. Next, copy the neck seam, excluding any add-on ribbing, by lifting the trim and out-

---

TIP

Because knits are often spongy or bulky, pinning a paper pattern to the fabric can easily tear standard pattern tissue. Instead, use pattern weights or pin the pattern just through the upper fabric layer.

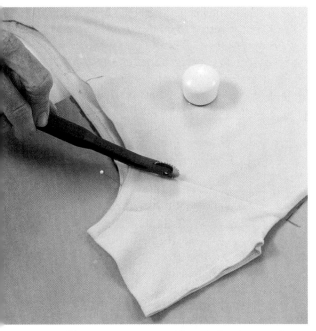

To copy an armscye, either lift the sleeve and outline the seam or run a spoked tracing wheel along the armscye, then add the seam allowance.

After outlining the front and back neckline on pattern paper, add seam allowances and cut both layers of paper to the higher neckline. Next, trim half the pattern to the lower neckline.

To make a full-sleeve pattern, fold the pattern paper in half, and place the sleeve on top of it, lining up the sleeve fold to the paper fold. Outline the sleeve, then add seam and hem allowances.

If a garment has facings, make a separate front and back facing pattern by copying each neckline onto pattern paper using the main pattern piece. Use a ruler to mark the facing width on the pattern.

lining the seam or by running a tracing wheel along the seam. Copy both the front and back neckline onto the same pattern.

4. If there is a hem, mark the finished hemline. If there is ribbing at the bottom, mark the seamline.

5. After removing the T-shirt, add the seam allowances and the hem allowance. You may add ¼ in. or more as a seam allowance, depending on the knit you are using and how you plan to finish the seams.

6. At the neckline, cut both layers of paper to the higher neckline, which is typically the back neckline, then trim half of the pattern to the lower neckline (see the top right photo on p. 25).

7. Next, make a full sleeve pattern by folding the pattern paper in half lengthwise. Place the T-shirt sleeve on top of the pattern paper, lining up the sleeve fold to the pattern fold.

8. Outline the sleeve, and mark the sleeve cap by lifting the T-shirt near the seam or by running a spoked tracing wheel along the armscye. Add the seam allowance and hem allowance (see the bottom left photo on p. 23).

9. Write the amount of the seam allowance and hem allowance on the pattern, as well as the finished width of the ribbed trim or binding. Follow the directions on pp. 56-59 to determine how wide and how long to cut the neck trim.

10. If the T-shirt has facings, make separate front and back facing patterns by copying the front and back necklines onto pattern paper, using the main pattern as a guide (see the bottom right photo on p. 23).

11. After outlining the center, neckline, and shoulder, measure the width of the finished facing on the garment, and add two seam allowances. Use the same amount of seam allowance you used on the main pattern. One seam allowance is needed for sewing the neckline and the other allows you to trim and neaten the inner facing edge during serging or before using a machine overlock or zigzag stitch. To mark the curved facing's cutting width, measure from the neckline down at close intervals.

TIP

Useful tools to have for sewing knits include a Teflon soleplate for your iron and a walking foot for sewing bulky fabrics or those with a nap.

SELECTING INTERFACING AND NOTIONS

Successful sewing projects rely on choosing the best or most appropriate interfacing and notions. Compatible interfacing, stretch needles, strong and elastic thread, and specialty elastics help you accomplish professional results.

Interfacing certain areas of knit garments can control stretching and help the garment retain its shape.

Interfacing

Interfacing is useful in certain areas of knit garments to control stretching and help retain the shape. You would think that stretchy fabrics would need interfacings that stretch, but that is not always the case. Styles that have facings are not meant to stretch at the facing edge. Facings and therefore interfacings are used on stable to moderately stretchy knits that have a neckline large enough to fit over the head without stretching or that have a button or zipper closure.

To stabilize neckline facings, which helps to retain the neckline shape and avoid popped stitches, use lightweight stable interfacings. Nonwoven interfacing is best for small areas like these that need maximum stability. This is one of the few situations where I prefer using nonwoven fusible interfacings because they are easy to use, come in a variety of weights and firmnesses, preserve the shape of the neckline, and control stretching.

Styles with larger facings are different. On a cardigan style for example, it is best

TIP

Small pieces of fusible tricot interfacing have many useful applications. Use narrow lengthwise strips to control stretching on vertical in-seam pockets and shoulder seams, or use narrow crosswise strips to control the hem edge.

to control the crosswise stretch but not the lengthwise stretch because eventually the garment will grow a bit lengthwise and a very stable interfacing would cause pulling at the lower front hem. You should stabilize larger areas by using a more supple knitted interfacing, such as the fusible tricot interfacings called Easy Knit and Fusi Knit, to name just two. Tricot interfacings have crosswise stretch and little or no lengthwise stretch. For maximum results, use tricot interfacings sideways so that they stretch lengthwise on the garment. This way you can allow for some lengthwise stretch yet limit crosswise stretch in the garment neckline. Hems are different; here it is best to

Fusible interfacings stabilize edges and add subtle control to areas of a garment. Nonwoven fusible interfacings give maximum control in small areas of a garment, while fusible tricot interfacings stabilize edges softly.

cut the interfacing so that it stretches around the body just like the fashion fabric. Interfacing hems reduces curling in the fabric and improves the quality of your topstitching.

Other areas that need interfacing are collars, cuffs, and plackets. In these places either a woven or knitted interfacing will work, but I prefer a knitted interfacing because of its supple hand. Another fusible tricot interfacing called So Sheer is nice to use when you need a very lightweight interfacing. Like other tricots, So Sheer stretches crosswise and not lengthwise, but it is semisheer. This makes it inconspicuous on lightweight knits and pastel colors, but it is also fine to use on opaque and dark fabrics. When you want to use the thinnest interfacing possible, use So Sheer instead of Easy Knit or Fusi Knit.

Peripheral facings, such as armhole and hem facings on stable knits stretching ½ in. or less for every 4 in., do not have to be interfaced, but neckline facings always benefit from interfacing.

Sew-in interfacing also has its uses. Use sew-in interfacing when the heat and pressure of fusing interfacing to the fabric is a problem because of the fiber content or texture. See how to stabilize facing seams without using interfacing on fabrics that drape on pp. 113-121.

Needles and Threads

Most knits can be sewn beautifully using a universal-point needle and good-quality, long-staple polyester thread. A universal-point needle has a slightly rounded tip that is suitable for sewing a variety of knits and woven fabrics. In some cases, however, you may want to use a ballpoint or stretch needle, both of which have rounded tips that penetrate the fabric without piercing the fabric yarns the way universal needles do. Change to a ballpoint or stretch needle to avoid skipped stitches when sewing densely knitted fabrics or to avoid snags when sewing fine or delicate stretch fabrics. These needles also give the best results when sewing on elastic.

For basic sewing, use 100% polyester or cotton-covered polyester. Woolly nylon thread is useful for creating soft seams on a serger and adding elasticity to seams on a sewing machine when used in the bobbin. Universal-point needles work well on most knits, but switch to ballpoint or stretch needles to avoid snags and skipped stitches on delicate, dense, or highly elastic fabrics.

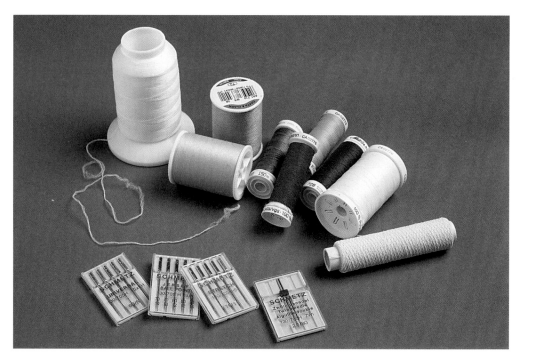

Needles come in a wide range of sizes from 60/8, suitable for very fine knits, to 90/14, suitable for thick, bulky, or heavy knits. Needle guidelines apply to both conventional sewing-machine needles and serger needles.

Double and triple needles make it easy to sew professional-looking multiple rows of topstitching. These needles have two or three needles on one shank and are labeled according to needle type, size, and width of spacing. A size 2,0/75 double needle has two size 75 needles spaced 2mm apart. A size 3,0/80 triple needle has three size 80 needles with the space between the two outer needles being 3mm. Multiple needles come in universal, ballpoint, and stretch versions.

Because knits need strong and elastic seams, use a good-quality, long-staple polyester or cotton-covered polyester thread when sewing on a conventional sewing machine. Both threads are also available on cones for use in a serger. When sewing fine knits like tricot, use very fine thread such as lingerie thread. Lingerie thread is typically nylon and comes in black and white.

Woolly nylon thread may be used in the upper looper or both the upper and lower loopers of a serger to create soft and elastic seams. It also works well in the bobbin of a conventional sewing machine when topstitching with a double or triple needle. Elastic sewing thread is another specialty thread that I like to use in the bobbin to add elasticity to a hemline or to serve as a stabilizer for buttonholes instead of gimp (see pp. 78-79).

Fine ballpoint pins are best for delicate knits, and T pins are useful for specialty knits that are bulky, loosely knitted, or textured.

Elastic

Knitwear styles are conducive to using elastic finishes that stretch with the garment. There are various types of basic and special-purpose elastics that have different characteristics suitable for specific applications.

The various types of basic and special-purpose elastics help you achieve professional results. Shown from left to right are woven elastic, braided elastic, two kinds of nonroll elastic, swimsuit elastic, knitted elastic, drawcord elastic, felt-back lingerie elastic, basic lingerie elastic, picot edge lingerie elastic, foldover lingerie elastic, stretch-lace lingerie elastic, and clear elastic.

Basic elastic   Basic or multipurpose elastics are meant to be covered by the fashion fabric and can either be inserted or stitched into the casing. These elastics may be braided, woven, or knitted. Braided elastic is firm and well suited for casing applications such as waistbands, legbands, and sleeve edges because it holds its shape. Nonroll waistband elastic is also braided and will not roll or fold over when stretched. Another braided elastic is swimwear elastic, which is treated to resist chlorine and salt water. The second type of basic elastic is woven elastic. It is stable and suitable for casing and stitched-in-place applications.

Knitted elastic comes in a wide range of widths and is very soft, making it best suited for stitching to the garment. One type of sew-through knitted waistband elastic has ⅛-in.-wide rows, or spaces without elastic, to facilitate stitching in place. Draw-cord elastic is a very useful knitted waistband elastic that has a cord knitted to the center that expands to become a draw-

string after you install the elastic. You can also use wide, colorful elastic trim on the outside of your garment.

Lingerie elastic   There are three types of lingerie elastic. Basic lingerie elastic comes in a variety of fashion colors and widths and is pretty enough to be applied to the outside of lingerie. Felt-back lingerie elastic comes in various widths and neutral colors and has a soft, plushy backing that is comfortable next to your skin. Both of these types of lingerie elastics often have a picot edge on one or both edges and are stitched in place rather than enclosed in a casing.

The third type of lingerie elastic folds over and encloses a garment edge. Foldover elastic is available in fashion colors and is often used to finish necklines and edges with a narrow binding on both lingerie and nonlingerie applications.

Stretch lace   Stretch lace trim is a soft and decorative elastic that is used on the outside of a garment as a way to finish a neckline, armhole, waistline, or edge. It is available in a variety of widths and in both neutral and fashion colors. When used on the outside of a garment, stretch lace trim is most frequently used on lingerie, bodysuits, and T-shirts. It also may be used as a neckline facing on knits and wovens.

Clear elastic   Clear elastic is thin, lightweight, and comes in various widths. It works best in a stitched-in-place application rather than in a casing because it has a tendency to fold back or roll. Clear elastic is very useful for stabilizing necklines, seams, and hems.

PREPARING THE FABRIC

Knits shrink more than wovens and have a one-way nap that results in subtle shading on plain knits and obvious shading on napped pile knits such as velvet. These two things affect the amount of fabric that you buy. Because of the variety of knits and

Steam dry-clean-only knits on a flat surface without touching the iron to the fabric.

This square of fabric has been washed and dried in the same way as the completed garment will be. When the laundered sample is compared with the outline, it shows considerable shrinkage.

TIP

I prefer not to prewash polyester or nylon knits because they do not shrink, and they are easier to cut with the fabric sizing still present.

---

fibers, it is difficult to predict how much shrinkage to expect. Most knits shrink more lengthwise than they do crosswise.

Washable knits must be preshrunk before cutting by washing and drying them in the same manner you plan to wash and dry the finished garment. To prevent unraveling when you prewash loosely woven knits, first sew a zigzag stitch or serge along the cut edge. Keep in mind that 100% cotton knits and rayon knits such as matte jersey continue to shrink after the first washing. This residual shrinkage can be kept to a minimum by washing and dry-

PRESSING KNITS

Knits require less pressing than wovens throughout the sewing process. In commercial sewing, most pressing is done at the end of construction to block the garment into shape, as you would a sweater. Fusible interfacing requires pressing of course, and pressing hems and edges is useful for the home sewer because a pressed edge is always easier to sew. But most knits don't press very well or fail to take a sharp crease when they do. Any crease is useful, but if you are sewing a knitted fabric that refuses to take a crease, measure and pin the hem allowance in place instead of pressing.

The way a knitted fabric presses depends primarily on its fiber content and stitch formation. When ironing, set the iron temperature according to the fiber content. Nylon and acetate are very sensitive to heat and damage easily, and acrylic is extremely susceptible to damage and distortion when pressed. When pressing nylon or acetate, keep in mind that leaving the iron in the same place for too long can be just as damaging as using a setting that is too hot. For acrylic, do as little pressing as possible. Steam the garment flat without touching the iron to the fabric, and be sure to let the fabric cool completely before moving the garment.

For best results, test everything, including how a fabric presses. ■

ing the fabric two or three times before cutting.

Dry-clean-only knits such as wool jersey and sweaterknits should be steamed on a flat surface. For best results, steam without touching the iron to the knit surface, and let the knit cool before moving the fabric. After steaming, leave the fabric flat for 24 hours before cutting to be sure the knit is completely dry and that it has had time to relax.

TIP

If a knit has a pressed-in lengthwise fold, it is probably permanent and you will need to refold the fabric to avoid placing this part of the fabric in a conspicuous place on the garment.

If you're not sure of a fabric's fiber content, if you have a mixture of different fibers in one fabric, or if washing is not recommended but you would like to wash the garment anyway, test-wash a sample of the fabric. To do a test wash, measure a 4-in. or 6-in. square of fabric, outline it on a piece of paper, then wash and dry it the way you plan to wash and dry the garment. Compare the sample with the original outline to see how much you can expect the fabric to shrink.

After test-washing a cotton knit sample, my 6-in. swatch shrank ¾ in. lengthwise but very little crosswise. After washing and drying the sample a second time, it shrank ¼ in. more, so I could conclude that this fabric would shrink about 6 in. per yard. When I buy knits, I typically allow ⅛ yd. more of fabric for every yard that I buy, but in this case it would be necessary to

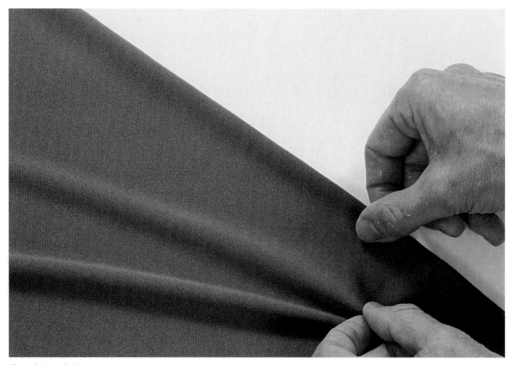

Fold fabric following a lengthwise rib, then measure the pattern grainlines to the folded edge because there are no actual selvages and the lengthwise edges that serve as selvages are often cut off grain.

increase that amount. Naturally, if you lengthen the pattern, you must also buy more fabric to allow for these adjustments.

LAYING OUT, CUTTING, AND MARKING THE FABRIC

You will notice that knitted fabrics do not have selvages. Knits have lengthwise ribs, or wales, and crosswise courses instead of lengthwise (warp) threads and crosswise (weft) threads. Circular knits come off a knitting machine as a cylindrical tube of fabric and are often cut open lengthwise for easier handling and sometimes stabilized to cut down on curling at the edges. Never assume that the lengthwise cut edge has been cut on grain.

When you fold your fabric to do the layout, place a lengthwise rib of the knit along the foldline instead of lining up the lengthwise cut edges as you would the selvages on woven fabrics. The cut edges of a knit may not be straight or follow a rib. Measure any grainlines on the pattern to the folded edge, since that edge has the straight of grain, then square the crossgrain to the table or use an L square. Instead of cutting the crossgrain square and wasting fabric, draw a line. By doing this, pattern pieces can extend past the line where possible and necessary.

Although it is usually preferable to fold the fabric with right sides facing, I find it is best to fold single knits and sweatshirt knits with the right side out and wrong sides facing. This is because it is easier to fold on grain by placing the rib, which is only visible on the right side, along the edge. You should also fold knits with a nap or texture, such as velvet or terry, with the wrong sides fac-

This lamé runs easily, as you can see from the sample. Cut the garment so that the fabric runs up from the hem, since that is typically the area with the least amount of stress.

ing because it is easier to align the fabric grain. Pattern pieces should be placed on the fabric using a "with nap" layout.

Some knit fabrics run (dropping stitches like a stocking) in one lengthwise direction or both. Knits that run from both ends typically run more readily from the last course knitted. See if your fabric runs by stretching both crosswise edges, then lay out the pattern pieces so that the fabric runs toward areas of the garment that have the greatest stress. In most cases, the upper edge of the garment has the greatest stress so it is best to cut the fabric so it runs up from the hemline.

As you lay out the pattern or cut the fabric, never allow the fabric to hang off your cutting table. If the fabric is longer than the table, support the extra length by using the backs of two chairs or by folding the fabric at the end of the cutting table.

To hold the pattern pieces in place, use weights or fine pins. Confine pins to the outer edges on delicate knits and swimsuit fabrics to avoid snagging the fabric surface. When cutting, hold the fabric flat to the cutting surface and use a rotary cutter or sharp scissors. Never pull at the edges of the fabric when you cut with scissors because you will stretch the fabric from under the pattern and distort the cutting line.

When marking your fabric, cut notches going out if you are using a knit pattern

When cutting knits, be sure to keep the pattern and fabric flat on a table and avoid pulling or stretching the edges.

To mark openwork knits, use small pieces of masking tape or stick-on Pattern Pals instead of notches and dots.

with a ¼-in. seam allowance. Take short ⅛-in. clips if the seam allowance is ⅝ in. wide. It is best to use a fabric marker to mark notches on loosely woven sweater-knits because they unravel easily and notches would be difficult or impossible to find along the edge.

Wax or clay tailor's chalk is very useful for marking on different textures of fabric. Wax marks steam out on wool and cotton but leave grease marks on synthetics and silk. Clay marks must be brushed or washed away. I prefer to use only white wax tailor's chalk and white or pale pastels in the clay type.

Air-erasable pens are very useful on white or light colors of all fabric types, but the marks may disappear sooner than you would like. You can avoid losing the marks

by waiting until you are ready to sew the garment before you mark. Use all markers sparingly, especially when marking the right side of the fabric, and avoid pressing over marks because heat may make them permanent. Openwork knits can be a challenge to notch or mark. For those, use small pieces of masking tape to mark notches and dots, or use purchased stick-on marking symbols such as Pattern Pals.

> **TIP**
>
> When both sides of a knitted fabric look alike, such as interlock and double-knit fabrics do, mark the wrong side using transparent tape or masking tape.

3   Sewing Seams, Hems, Edges, and Waistbands

Techniques for sewing knits are the building blocks to working successfully with a variety of knitted fabrics. Because these fabrics vary wildly in their amounts of stretch, textures, weights, and thicknesses, the perfect technique for a fabric that stretches easily is different from one for a thick yet firm fabric or one that is loosely knitted or lacy.

This chapter discusses the best stitch combinations for sewing seams and hems and different ways to finish necklines using topstitching, shaped facings, and single or double binding. You will also find directions for sewing narrow binding using a binder attachment and how to make all kinds of elastic waistbands.

SEWING SEAMS

Stretch fabrics need seams that stretch. You can incorporate stretch by using combinations of stitches that have built-in elasticity. Since most knits either curl at the edges or do not hold a crease, seam allowances on knits are usually kept together and narrow.

Narrow seams are terrific for fabrics you don't press—the seam looks neat whether the seam allowance is pressed to one side or not—but those narrow seams must be strong. Pattern companies that specialize in patterns for knitwear, like Kwik Sew and Stretch and Sew, typically use a ¼-in. seam allowance. Most other commercial patterns use a ⅝-in. seam allowance that you have to trim after sewing the seam.

There are advantages to both approaches. The ¼-in. seam allowance is convenient and easier to sew if the fabric edge is tightly knitted and neat, but you must be careful to keep the fabric edges aligned as you sew to avoid gaps in the seam. A ⅝-in. seam allowance is better if the fabric is loosely knitted, bulky, or unravels easily because you can sew farther into the cloth where the fabric is more stable, then trim away the shaggy edges. The seam allowances on stable knits that hold a crease, such as wool double knit, can be pressed open and left unfinished because they stay in place and don't unravel. Seams that are pressed open should have a ⅝-in. seam allowance.

(continued on p. 40)

	SEAMS	HEMS	NECKLINES
Which Technique to Use for Each Fabric			
Single knits	Three- or four-thread serger stitch Machine-overlock stitch Double-stitch seams using a narrow zigzag plus a medium zigzag or a machine or serger overlock stitch	Topstitch using a single, double, or triple needle Topstitch using a 2mm-wide and 2mm-long zigzag stitch Machine-blind hem using a 2mm-wide and 2mm-long zigzag stitch Serger blind hem	Shaped facings Turn back and topstitch Binding Ribbing or self-fabric as ribbing Straight facings Single-fold bias tape
Double knits	Narrow zigzag stitch (.5mm to 1mm wide and 2.5mm long) or stretch stitch then press seams open Three-or four-thread serger stitch Machine-overlock stitch Mock flat-felled seams Flatlock	Topstitch using a single, double, or triple needle Machine- or serger-blind hem Hand-blind hem using a blind catchstitch Flatlock	Shaped facings Single-layer binding Ribbing Turn back and topstitch
Interlock	Three- or four-thread serger stitch Machine-overlock stitch Double-stitch seams using a narrow zigzag plus a medium zigzag or machine or serger overlock stitch	Topstitch using a single, double, or triple needle Topstitch using a 2mm-wide and 2mm-long zigzag stitch Machine-blind hem using a 2mm-wide and 2mm-long zigzag stitch Serger-blind hem	Shaped facings Binding Ribbing or self-fabric as ribbing Turn back and topstitch with or without clear elastic Straight facings
Sweatshirt knits	Three- or four-thread serger stitch Machine-overlock stitch Flatlock Double-stitch seams using a narrow zigzag plus a medium zigzag or machine or serger overlock stitch	Topstitch using a single, double, or triple needle Topstitch using a 2mm-wide and 2mm-long zigzag stitch Flatlock Machine-blind hem using a 2mm-wide and 2mm-long zigzag stitch Serger-blind hem Hand-blind hem using a blind catchstitch	Turn back and topstitch Shaped facings Ribbing Single-layer binding Straight facings

	SEAMS	HEMS	NECKLINES
Ribbed knits	Three- or four-thread serger stitch Machine-overlock stitch Double-stitch seams using a narrow zigzag plus a medium zigzag or machine or serger overlock stitch	Topstitch using a single, double, or triple needle and woolly nylon or elastic thread in the bobbin Topstitch using a medium zigzag (2mm to 3mm wide and long) Blind hem on a machine using a 2mm-wide and 2mm-long zigzag or on a serger Flatlock Machine or serger lettuce edge	Ribbing Single-layer binding Turn back and topstitch with or without elastic Narrow binding using a binder attachment
Swimsuit fabrics and stretch lace	Three-thread serger stitch (woolly nylon in loopers is useful) Machine-overlock, stretch-overlock, or double-overlock stitch Double-stitch seams using a 1mm-wide and 2mm-long zigzag stitch plus a 2mm to 3mm-wide-and-long zigzag or a machine or serger overlock stitch	Topstitch using a single, double, or triple needle and woolly nylon in the bobbin Topstitch using a medium zigzag (2mm to 3mm wide and long) Machine or serger lettuce edge	Turn back and topstitch with or without elastic Self-binding Self-fabric as ribbing Stretch lace trim or lingerie elastic Narrow binding using a binder attachment
Stretch velvets (These are cut with a ½-in. or ⅝-in. seam allowance. A walking foot is very useful here.)	Three- or four-thread serger stitch and adjust the differential feed Machine-overlock stitch, place on seamline, and trim after stitching Double-stitch seams using a narrow zigzag stitch (.5mm to 1mm wide and 2.5mm long) plus a medium zigzag or machine or serger overlock stitch Baby serger stitch or sheer-cut velvets	Topstitch using a single, double, or triple needle Topstitch using a medium zigzag (2mm to 3mm wide and long) Hand-blind hem using a blind catchstitch Serger-blind hem Machine-blind hem using a 2mm-wide and 2mm-long zigzag stitch and a blind-hem foot	Turn back and topstitch with or without elastic Single-layer binding Shaped facings Ribbing or self-fabric as ribbing
Stretch chenille (These are cut with a ½-in. or ⅝-in. seam allowance. A walking foot is very useful here.)	Three- or four-thread serger stitch and adjust the differential feed Machine-overlock stitch, place on seamline, and trim after stitching Double-stitch seams using a 1mm-wide and 2.5mm-long zigzag combined with a zigzag that is 3mm, 4mm, or 5mm wide and 2mm long	Topstitch using a medium-to-wide zigzag (2.5mm to 4mm wide and long) Serger-blind hem Machine-blind hem using a 2mm-wide and 5mm-long zigzag stitch and a blind-hem foot Hand-blind hem using a blind catchstitch	Turn back and topstitch with or without elastic Shaped facings Ribbing Single-layer binding or narrow binding; use a binder attachment with jersey or tricot; either decorative or turned to the inside of the garment and topstitched *(continued on p. 38)*

	SEAMS	HEMS	NECKLINES
Stretch terry (These are cut with a ½-in. or ⅝-in. seam allowance. A walking foot is useful if the fabric is thick.)	Three- or four-thread serger stitch Machine-overlock stitch, place on seamline, and trim after stitching Double-stitch seams using a 1mm-wide and 2.5mm-long zigzag combined with a zigzag that is 3mm, 4mm, or 5mm wide and 2mm long Mock flat-felled seam	Topstitch using a single or double needle Topstitch using a medium-to-wide zigzag (2.5mm to 4mm wide and long) Serger-blind hem Machine-blind hem using a 2mm-wide and 5mm-long zigzag stitch and a blind-hem foot	Turn back and topstitch with or without elastic Shaped facings Single-layer binding, or use a binder attachment with jersey or tricot Ribbing
Sweaterknits and sweaterbodies (These are cut with a ½-in. or ⅝-in. seam allowance. A walking foot is useful if the fabric is bulky.)	Three- or four-thread serger stitch and adjust differential feed Machine-overlock stitch, place on seamline, and trim after sewing Double-stitch seams using a narrow-to-medium zigzag (.5mm to 2mm wide and 2.5mm long) plus a medium-to-wide zigzag (2mm to 5mm wide and 3mm long) or a machine or serger overlock stitch	Serger-blind hem Hand-blind hem using a blind catchstitch Machine-blind hem using a 2mm-wide and 2mm- to 5mm-long zigzag and a blind-hem foot Topstitch using a single, double, or triple needle Bind off the fabric Flatlock	Ribbing or self-fabric as ribbing Binding (self-fabric or purchased trim) Turn back and topstitch with or without elastic Shaped facings Machine-made couched yarn trim Unravel the fabric and hand-knit or crochet a trim
Raschel knit (Very open and lacey variety. These are cut with a ½-in. or ⅝-in. seam allowance.)	Double-stitch seams using a narrow-to-medium zigzag (1mm to 2.5mm wide and long) plus a three- or four-thread serger stitch, a machine overlock stitch, or a second row of zigzag stitching	Topstitch using double or triple needles Topstitch using a medium-to-wide zigzag (2mm to 3mm wide and long)	Apply elastic, then turn back and topstitch Self-binding or contrasting binding fabric If using a narrow binding applied with a binder, use a zigzag stitch to sew in place Ribbing
Synthetic fleece	Three- or four-thread serger stitch and adjust differential feed Machine-overlock stitch Double-stitch seams using a narrow-to-medium zigzag (.5mm to 2mm wide and 2.5mm long depending on the lengthwise stretch) plus a medium-to-wide zigzag (2mm to 5mm wide and 3mm long) or a machine or serger overlock stitch	Turn back and topstitch using a single, double, or triple needle Topstitch using a medium to-wide zigzag stitch Topstitch using a decorative stitch Ribbing Serger-blind hem	Turn back and topstitch Binding (self-fabric, other fabric, or purchased trim) Shaped facings (self-fabric or other fabric)

	SEAMS	HEMS	NECKLINES
Synthetic fleece (*continued*)	Mock flat-felled seams Decorative lapped seams Flatlock	Machine-blind hem using a 2mm-wide and 2mm-long zigzag stitch and a blind-hem foot Binding Flatlock	
Slinky knits (These are cut with a ½-in. or ⅝-in. seam allowance.)	Three- or four-thread serger stitch and adjust the differential feed Machine-overlock stitch, place on seamline, and trim after stitching Double-stitch seams using a narrow-to-medium zigzag stitch (1mm to 2mm wide and 2.5mm long) plus a wider zigzag or a serger or machine overlock stitch	Topstitch using a double or triple needle Topstitch tight garments with a medium zigzag stitch (2mm to 3mm wide and long) Lettuce edge	Turn back and topstitch with or without elastic Self-fabric as ribbing Single-layer binding Narrow binding using a binder attachment
Matte jersey (These are cut with a ½-in. or ⅝-in. seam allowance.)	Three- or four-thread serger stitch and adjust the differential feed Double-stitch seams using a narrow zigzag (.5mm to 2mm wide and 2mm long) plus a medium zigzag or a serger or machine overlock stitch Baby serger stitch for lightweight fabrics	Topstitch using a single, double, or triple needle Topstitch using a medium zigzag (2mm to 3mm wide and long) Hand-blind hem using a blind catchstitch Scalloped hem Picot hem Lettuce edge	Turn back and topstitch with or without elastic Shaped facings Straight facings Single-layer binding Narrow binding using a binder attachment Self-fabric as ribbing Purchased single-fold bias tape

GETTING THE BEST STITCH

Whether you are sewing on a conventional machine or on a serger, always check the needle size and the condition of the needle, then sew a sample of the type of stitch and stitch setting that you are planning to use. Often you will have many stitches to choose from that produce good results. At other times, you may need to modify the stitch length or the stitch width.

If the stitch setting is too short, the seam looks stretched or wavy. If the stitch is too long, the seam looks puckered and the stitches will "pop" when you pull the seam. If the stitch is too wide, it will crease or "tunnel" the fabric. When you find a setting variation that works well on a fabric, it's a good idea to write it down or, better yet, mark and save the actual sample. This way you'll have an easy reference when you need it.

There are several ways that you can sew a seam. You can use a narrow zigzag stitch, two rows of zigzagging, or an overlock stitch on a sewing machine. Other methods are using a mock flat-felled seam or serging a seam.

Narrow Zigzag Stitch

An easy way to add elasticity to a seam is to use a narrow zigzag instead of a straight stitch. On stable knits such as jersey, use a 0.5mm stitch width and a 2.5mm stitch length. Increase the width and shorten the length to increase the elasticity. For an elastic seam on interlock or double knits, try setting the stitch width to 1mm and the stitch length to 1.5mm.

Another option is to use the basic stretch stitch that is now included on most sewing machines. This is a highly elastic stitch that is just another narrow zigzag variation. Depending on the settings you use, the basic stretch stitch tends to work better on firm knits than it does on knits that have a lot of stretch. Seams may be pressed open with all these zigzag variations, or they may be trimmed and stitched with a second row of stitches.

Double-Stitched Seam Combinations

Most seams are best stitched together twice, both for strength and to keep the seam allowances together and neat. You can use either two rows of a narrow zigzag, or you can use a narrow zigzag plus a medium or wide zigzag for the second row of stitches. In both cases, stitch the first row on the seamline and the second row approximately ⅛ in. away. A medium zigzag, using a 2mm setting for both the stitch width and length, is best for thin or lightweight knits. Use a wider zigzag on firmer or thicker knits—a 3mm, 4mm, or even 5mm setting for the stitch width and a length of 2.5mm or more. Trim the seam allowance next to the second row of stitches.

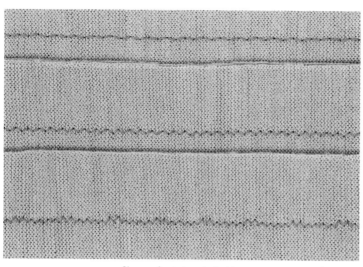

Shown from top to bottom are a narrow zigzag 0.5mm wide and 2.5mm long, a narrow zigzag 1mm wide and 1.5mm long, and a basic stretch stitch.

Here are three double-stitched seam combinations (from top to bottom: two rows of narrow zigzag stitch, a narrow zigzag plus a medium zigzag stitch, and a narrow zigzag plus a machine overlock stitch.

Overlock and Stretch-Overlock Stitches

Sewing-machine overlock stitches imitate serger stitches and serve two functions: first to sew the seam, then to finish the edge, all in one step. Because knits are so popular, your machine doesn't have to be the top of the line to include these utility stitches.

The overlock stitch is excellent for sewing lightweight jersey and tricot, while the double-overlock stitch is terrific on firm and coarse-knitted fabrics such as swimwear and sweaterknits. The stretch overlock is a versatile stitch just right for sewing swimwear and a variety of soft or looser-knitted fabrics. It can also be used for flat-joining seams on terry and velour. Flat-joined seams are sewn by overlapping the seam allowances instead of sewing them with right sides together. Use this kind of seam to avoid ridges and chafing on activewear such as bicycle shorts or to reduce bulk on loopy fabrics.

Overlock stitches are meant to be used along the outer edge of the fabric, so if you have allowed a ⅝-in. seam allowance, trim it to ¼ in. before sewing the seam. When sewing, use an overlock foot (also called an over-the-edge foot) to prevent the stitches from squeezing the edge of the fabric and to create a smooth edge. I also like to use the basic overlock stitch as an edge finish or as a second row of stitches, first sewing the seam with a narrow zigzag stitch, then trimming the seam allowance to ¼ in. and overlocking the edges together. On bulky, loosely knitted, or unstable edges, it is best to first sew with a double-overlock or stretch-overlock stitch along the ⅝-in. seamline using a standard foot, then trim away the excess seam.

Mock Flat-Felled Seams

The mock flat-felled seam is a good option on fabrics that do not unravel easily and when reducing bulk is useful or necessary.

1. *To make a mock flat-felled seam, start by sewing the seam with right sides facing and using a ⅝-in. seam allowance.*

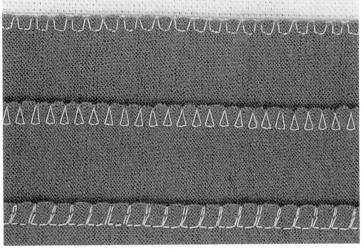

Machine overlock stitches include (from top to bottom) a basic overlock, a double overlock, and a stretch overlock.

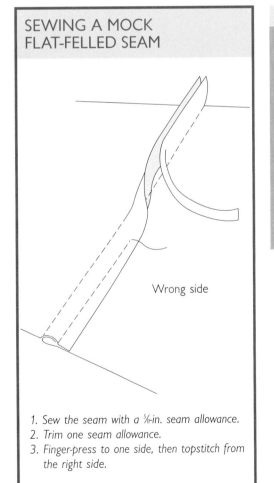

SEWING A MOCK FLAT-FELLED SEAM

Wrong side

1. Sew the seam with a ⅝-in. seam allowance.
2. Trim one seam allowance.
3. Finger-press to one side, then topstitch from the right side.

TIP

Sometimes it's good to use a machine overlock stitch instead of a serger because a machine is already threaded with matching thread and all you need to do is change the stitch setting.

2. Next, trim one seam allowance to ⅛ in. or
   ¼ in., then finger-press the wider seam
   allowance to cover the trimmed seam.
3. Topstitch the seam from the right side,
   lining up the outer edge of the presser foot
   to the original seam. Finally, trim the
   excess seam allowance on the wrong side of
   the garment next to the stitching.

*Basic serger seams
include (from top to
bottom) a three-
thread serger seam
using the right
needle, a three-
thread serger seam
using the left needle,
and a four-thread
serger seam.*

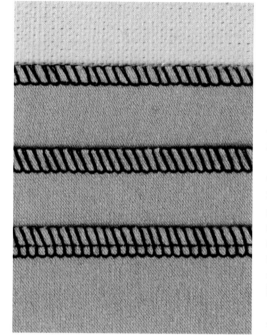

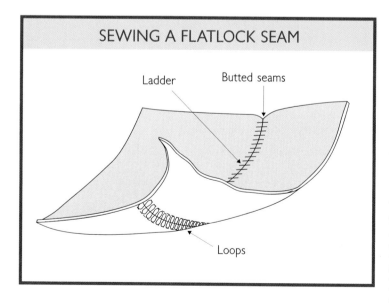

SEWING A FLATLOCK SEAM

Ladder Butted seams

Loops

Serger Seams

Serger seams are perfect for knits because
they are narrow and neat. They are also fast
and easy because you trim the seam
allowance, sew the seam, and finish the
edge in one step. Although most sergers
have the capacity to use two, three, four, or
five threads, the three- and four-thread
capacities are the most useful when sewing
seams on knits. A three-thread seam is more
elastic than a four-thread seam so it should
be used on more elastic knits. Use the right
needle of the serger to sew a narrow three-
thread seam on thin or lightweight knits,
and use the left needle to sew a three-thread
seam on thick or bulky knits or to create a
wider seam. A four-thread seam is more
stable and secure than a three-thread seam
so it is best for stable knits.

A baby serger stitch is a narrow, more
delicate three-thread stitch that is perfect
for very lightweight knits, tricot, and
sheers, such as stretch chiffon, stretch illusion, and tulle. Using a three-thread serger
stitch with the right needle engaged and
the additional stitch fingers removed (as
you would for a rolled hem) creates the
baby serger stitch.

A serger can also sew flatlock seams,
which are butted and therefore flat. They
are especially useful on thick knits that do
not unravel easily, such as sweatshirt knits
and synthetic fleece. They are also interesting to use on thinner knits if you want a
decorative topstitched look. The stitch
forms loops on the top side and a ladder on
the bottom side. Stitching the fabric with
wrong sides together places the serger loops
on the outside of the garment, while stitching the fabric with right sides together
places the ladder on the outside of the garment (see the illustration at left).

To create a flatlock seam, sew the same
way as you would a three-thread seam, but
make the following adjustments. Loosen
the needle tension to zero, then tighten the
lower looper until the loops completely disappear. You only need to adjust the upper
looper if the seam won't flatten or if the
fabric is thick. After sewing the seam, pull

TIP

Flatlock seams take on a decorative look when you use contrasting or decorative thread in the upper looper.

hem allowance according to the silhouette of the garment and the amount of curl in the knit.

Blind Hems by Hand or Machine

You can sew hems invisibly by hand using a blind catchstitch or by machine using a blind-hemming stitch or zigzag stitch together with a blindstitch foot. A machine blind-hemming stitch is a durable hem stitch meant to duplicate a hand-sewn blind hem. It works beautifully on thick or spongy fabrics, but it can be too obvious on thinner knits.

To sew a hem by hand using a blind catchstitch, press up the garment hem allowance, and pin or machine-baste it. Fold back the hem edge ¼ in. to ½ in. from the cut edge, then sew the blind catchstitch from left to right with the needle pointing left (see the illustration below). Alternate taking a small stitch in the garment hem with taking the smallest stitch possible in the garment.

A standard machine blind-hemming stitch works well on knits that are stable or have little stretch. When you need more stretch, a simple zigzag stitch works well because it is stretchy, its spacing is more

TIP

Cutting a cross-wise strip of fusible tricot interfacing, then fusing it to the hem allowance helps reduce curling.

the two fabric layers apart until the seam lies flat. If you want to flatlock fabric that unravels, fold the seam allowance out of the way, and flatlock the folded edges without cutting the fold.

SEWING HEMS

Hems can be sewn invisibly by hand or machine, or they can be topstitched using single or multiple rows of stitching. Most knits have topstitched hems that are obvious and visible. The hem allowance for knits can range from ⅜ in. to 1½ in. wide. Knits that curl easily to the outside, like single knits, jersey, and tricot, do best when the hem allowance is between 1 in. and 1½ in. wide. On garments that flare at the bottom, keep the hems narrow. To get the best results, always adjust the size of the

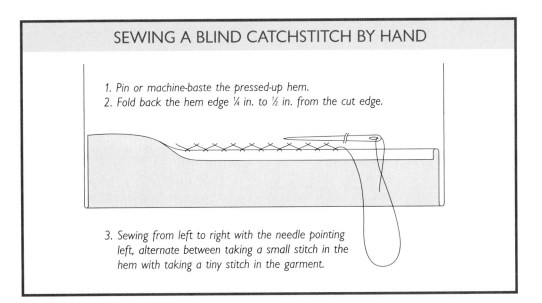

SEWING A BLIND CATCHSTITCH BY HAND

1. Pin or machine-baste the pressed-up hem.
2. Fold back the hem edge ¼ in. to ½ in. from the cut edge.

3. Sewing from left to right with the needle pointing left, alternate between taking a small stitch in the hem with taking a tiny stitch in the garment.

compatible with knitted fabrics, and it results in a neater edge.

1. *Start by choosing either the standard blind-hemming stitch or the zigzag stitch. Set the width and length to 2mm, but be ready to fine-tune.*
2. *Press up the hem allowance, then fold the garment back on itself to expose about ¼ in. of hem.*
3. *Align the fold under the presser foot, allowing the needle to catch only a yarn or two of the fold, and adjust the stitch width to take the smallest bite into the fabric. Use the finest needle you can so that the stitch will be as unnoticeable as possible on the right side. Increasing the stitch length and loosening the tension will also help you tailor the setting to the fabric you are sewing. Increasing the stitch length makes the stitches farther apart and is useful on thicker knits such as synthetic fleece. Loosening the tension reduces dimpling on the right side of the garment.*

Topstitched Hems Using Single, Double, or Triple Needles

Topstitched hems are durable and suitable for many different types of garments. Double and triple needles make it easy to sew perfect parallel rows, with topstitching on the outside and zigzag stitching on the inside. Multineedle topstitching is more elastic than using a single row of straight stitching because of the zigzag on the back side. These needles are available with various widths between the needles and in a range of sizes and types, including stretch needles. Thick and stable knits look best with a wide spread between the needles, but thin and lightweight knits look best when the needles are closer together, which avoids or reduces the ridge that can form between the needles.

You can use a single row of single-needle straight stitching if the knitted fabric is stable and the hem does not need to stretch, or you can use a single row of zigzag stitching to increase the amount of stretch in the hem. Start with a medium-size zigzag setting that is 2mm wide and long, but

Topstitched hems are suitable for a variety of fabrics and styles. Single-needle straight stitching is best for stable fabrics and hems that do not need to stretch. To sew more elastic hems, use a zigzag stitch or multineedle topstitching. Shown from left to right are a zigzag stitch, a straight stitch, a double needle, and a triple needle.

increase the width and length when sewing bulky fabrics.

To topstitch a hem, work from the right side of the garment using a seam allowance that is about ¼ in. narrower than the hem allowance. Start sewing at a side seam, and overlap the stitching at the end by two stitches. For neat starts and stops, lock in the stitch by sewing in place, either by dropping the feed dogs or by reducing the stitch length and width to zero.

Serged Hems

The nice thing about a serger blind hem is that as it hems the garment, it also finishes the hem edge, trimming it away. For most sergers, an adjustable blindstitch foot is available, which makes the blindstitch feature easier to use because of the guide plate. With the hem in place under the foot, adjust the guide plate so the hem fold lines up with the needle.

Blind hem   To sew a basic serger blind hem, set your machine for two- or three-thread serging, using the right-hand needle. Fold up and position the hem as you would for a machine blind-hemming stitch so that the serger needle catches only a thread or two of the fabric. The blade will trim the hem edge, and the serger loopers will hem and clean-finish it. Use a long stitch-length setting of 4mm so the stitches are not close together.

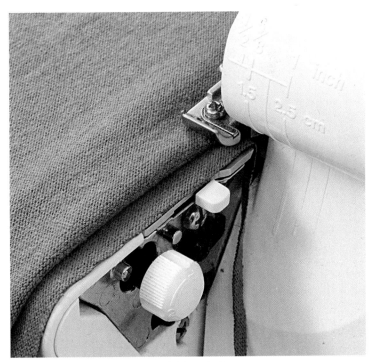

To sew a blind hem on a serger, fold up the hem and position it under the presser foot as you would for a machine blind hem, making sure that the needle catches only a thread or two of fabric.

TIP

Reducing the needle thread tension makes the blind-hemming stitch less obvious on the right side.

A false blind hem looks like a sewn-on band, but it is sewn in the same position as a standard blind hem. Use a standard-length three-thread serger stitch, and position the fold so that the needle sews farther in to the hem fold than you would with a standard blind hem.

False blind hem   A false blind hem looks like a sewn-on band because the hem creates a seamline on the right side of the garment. A blindstitch foot is useful here as well. To sew a false blind hem, prepare the hem as you would for a standard blind hem. Align the fabric so that the needle just pierces the fold, then use a standard three-thread serger stitch with a length of 2.5mm so the band is held firmly in place. For a false blind hem, the needle should be farther into the hem fold than for a standard blind hem.

Flatlock hem   A flatlock hem stitch, just like a flatlock seam, is visible on the right side. To sew a flatlock hem, which works best on straight hems, adjust the tensions as described for a flatlock seam (see pp. 42-43). Prepare the hem by first pressing back the hem allowance. To have the loops on the

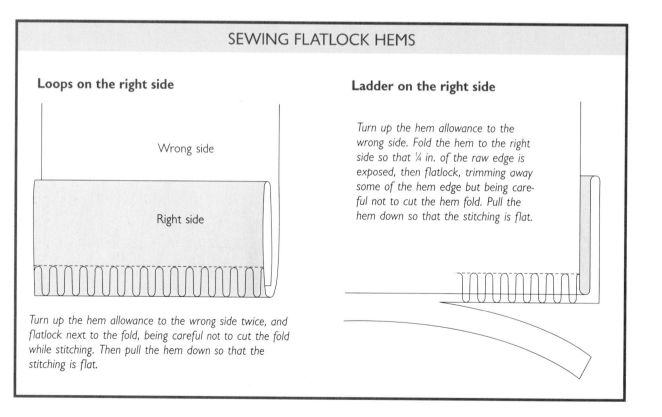

SEWING FLATLOCK HEMS

Loops on the right side

Wrong side

Right side

Turn up the hem allowance to the wrong side twice, and flatlock next to the fold, being careful not to cut the fold while stitching. Then pull the hem down so that the stitching is flat.

Ladder on the right side

Turn up the hem allowance to the wrong side. Fold the hem to the right side so that ¼ in. of the raw edge is exposed, then flatlock, trimming away some of the hem edge but being careful not to cut the hem fold. Pull the hem down so that the stitching is flat.

right side, turn up the hem to the wrong side again at the top of the hem edge (see the illustration at left on the facing page). This second fold encloses the hem edge. Next, flatlock from the right side, lining up the outer edge of the stitch to the fold and being careful not to cut the fold while stitching. Pull the hem down to flatten the stitches.

To have the ladder on the right side, fold the hem to the right side so that the fold is ¼ in. less than the hem allowance (the same position as a blind hem). Flatlock close to the fold, trimming some of the hem edge without cutting the fold (see the illustration at right on the facing page).

Other Edge Finishes for Lightweight Knits

Picot, shell, and lettuce edges are decorative finishes. These work well for soft and lightweight knits that have a moderate or

more amount of stretch, such as tricot, interlocks, stretch illusion, lightweight spandex knits, and matte jersey.

Picot edge   A fine picot edge is easy to do on a sewing machine using a wide zigzag stitch or an overlock stitch, which is a variation of a zigzag. In both cases, fold under the hem allowance. Place the fabric to the left of the presser foot, and position it so that the right swing of the needle goes a little past the folded edge. Start with a zigzag stitch width of 5mm and a length of 2mm, and try out the stitch to see if you like the spacing. A longer length creates a wider picot.

Shell edge   You can create a bolder scallop using the blind-hemming stitch of your sewing machine. Start by setting the stitch width to 5mm and the length to 1.5mm. If possible on your sewing machine, use the

You can sew a fine picot edge on lightweight fabrics by folding under the hem allowance and sewing a zigzag stitch along the hem fold. Start with a stitch setting that is 5mm wide and 2mm long, then vary the width or length to find the best setting for your fabric.

Create a bold scalloped edge on lightweight fabrics by sewing a machine blind-hemming stitch along the folded hem edge. Start with a stitch setting that is 5mm wide and 1.5mm long, then modify the setting to change the width and length of the scalloped edge.

mirror-image feature so that you can keep the fabric to the left of the presser foot as you sew. The right swing of the blind-hemming stitch should go slightly past the edge of the fabric. If you do not have the mirror-image feature, just sew with the fabric to the right of the foot so that the stitch swings past the edge of the hem to the left of the foot. Remember to always do a sample stitch. If you want to increase the space between the scallops, increase the stitch length.

Lettuce edge Flirty lettuce-leaf edges can be done easily by using a satin stitch on a sewing machine or by using a rolled hem on a serger.

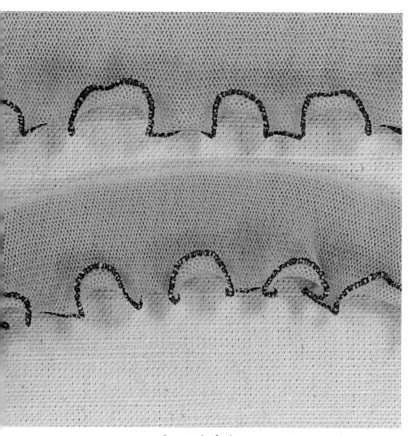

Lettuce-leaf edges are easy to sew either on a sewing machine using a satin stitch or on a serger using a rolled-hem stitch. You get the best results on light- to medium-weight knitted fabrics that have lots of stretch because stretch is necessary to create the curly leaf effect.

On a sewing machine, set the stitch width to a medium zigzag and the length to 1mm. The closely spaced stitch will stretch the fabric and ripple the edge. Press or fold under the hem allowance, then starting at a seam from the right side, sew a satin stitch along the fold, making sure the needle goes over the edge of the fabric on the right swing of the needle. Lastly, trim the excess hem allowance next to the satin stitch. You can stretch the edge after stitching to increase the fluted effect.

On a serger, using a narrow rolled hem or a nonrolled setting with negative differential feed to stretch the fabric as it sews will produce a lettuce edge. Increasing the number of stitches to the inch and the foot pressure increases the stretching. Consider using a decorative thread in the upper looper to play up the fluted edge.

SEWING NECKLINE AND EDGE FINISHES

You should select a neckline finish that is the most compatible with the thickness of the knit you are sewing, the degree of stretch in the fabric, and the style of the garment. Knit garments not only need seams and hems that stretch but also typically need necklines that stretch. Binding, ribbing, and elastic neckline finishes are usually interchangeable because they are all different ways to create stable edges that stretch. Use facings only when eliminating stretch is the objective. The methods described here for applying elastic can also be used to finish waistlines.

Turned and Stitched

The easiest way to finish curved necklines and armholes is by simply turning back the seam allowance and stitching it in place. A simple turned-and-stitched neckline finish is suitable for most knits. The exceptions are knits that unravel easily or have no stretch, such as raschel sweater-

knits, and knits that stretch out easily and don't recover well, such as some silk or chenille knits.

1. To use the turned-and-stitched method, start by cutting out the garment using a ½-in. to ⅝-in. seam allowance.
2. Sew the garment shoulder seams.

3. Serge the raw edges of the neckline and armholes if desired. It is not essential to do so because the topstitching will keep the raw edges in place and neat.
4. Press the seam allowance to the wrong side. Since most knits don't hold a crease very well, position pins perpendicular to the folded edge to hold the seam allowance in place.

TIP

Sewing a cross-wise test seam will help you determine how well the edge holds its shape.

For a turned-and-stitched neckline, press back or turn back and pin the seam allowance. Because knits don't hold a crease well, keep the seam allowance in place by inserting the pins perpendicular to the edge.

Single-needle topstitching can be used if the fabric is stable and does not unravel easily. Otherwise, using a single row of zigzag stitching or multineedle topstitching is more elastic and covers the raw edge on the wrong side of the neckline. Using a ¼-in. to ⅜-in. seam allowance, topstitch close to the raw edge.

5. *Starting at a shoulder seam, topstitch the neck edge from the right side using a medium zigzag stitch that is 2mm wide and 2mm long. You could also use double- or triple-needle topstitching. In all cases, topstitch using a ¼-in. to ⅜-in. seam allowance so the innermost stitch is close to the edge of the seam allowance.*

6. *Finally, sew the side seams, then topstitch the armholes starting at the side seams.*

Shaped Facings

You can use facings on necklines and edges that do not need to stretch. Shaped facings are a good way to finish necklines when sewing stable knits or knits with moderate stretch, such as jersey, interlock, and double knits, although these must be stabilized. To use facings on a garment, the neckline must be large enough to pull over the head without stretching, or it must have some kind of closure. Use fusible interfacing for facings because it is the easiest way to achieve professional results.

On washable garments, I like to topstitch the facings to the garment for practical and aesthetic reasons. The neckline looks attractive, and the facings always stay in place. On dry-cleaned garments, facings can be hand- or machine-tacked to the shoulder seams if you don't want topstitching, but they must be understitched to achieve a smooth neckline edge that rolls toward the inside.

To sew the facings:

1. *Cut the interfacing using the facing patterns, then fuse it in place on the wrong side of the facing following the manufacturer's recommendations.*

2. *Next, sew the seams in one of three ways. You could sew the facing shoulder seams, trim the seam allowances to ¼ in., and press the seams open, or you could double-stitch the seams, then trim and press them to one side in the opposite direction of the garment seams. You could also use a machine or serger overlock stitch and press to one side.*
3. *Finish the facing's unnotched edge, or outer curve, using a medium zigzag stitch or a machine or serger overlock stitch.*

To attach the facings to the garment:

1. *Pin the facing to the garment neckline with right sides facing, then use a straight stitch to sew with the facing on top.*
2. *On most knits, trim the neck seam to ¼ in. and clip the seam allowances at the curves and corners. On double knits and other bulky knits, grade the seam allowances by cutting the facing seam allowance to ¼ in. and the garment seam allowance to ⅜ in.*

3. *Press the seam allowances toward the facing, and if you are not going to use top-stitching, understitch the neckline. Understitch with the right side of the facing up, being sure to catch the seam allowances and stay ⅛ in. away from the neck seam.*
4. *Starting at a back seam or shoulder seam, topstitch the neckline from the right side of the garment. Topstitch either near the neckline edge or, better still, as close as possible to the facing's finished edge to keep the entire facing flat and in place. When top-stitching close to the facing's finished edge, it is best to machine-baste the facing in place to prevent the fabric layers from shifting.*

TIP

If you want to keep armhole and hem facings as soft as possible, you do not have to interface them, but the fabric must be very stable to have successful results.

Finish the shaped facing's unnotched edge or outer curve using a zigzag stitch or a machine or serger overlock stitch.

Understitching stitches the seam allowance to the facing and helps keep the edge neat and flat. Be sure to understitch with the right side facing up.

A binder attachment has been my favorite machine accessory since I started using it with knitted fabrics. Using bias wovens or, better yet, lightweight knits cut on the crossgrain, you can apply single binding to cover the raw edges of a garment in one step. The binder feeds and folds the binding fabric along both cut edges and down the center to enclose the neckline edge just before reaching the presser foot. Then it edgestitches the binding close to the upper fold. You can also use a binder to finish sleeve plackets, to bind a keyhole neckline, and to make button loops, belt loops, shoulder straps, and narrow ties. Once you start using it, you will continue to find other uses.

1. To use a binder attachment, cut the fabric to form a point at the center to facilitate feeding the binding fabric through the binder when you begin.

2. Using a long pin or an awl, slide the fabric toward the presser foot and under the needle (see the photo at left below). Pull the binding fabric back and forth through the binder to align the fabric so the folds are even on both sides. You will have more control if you sew the binding for a few inches before inserting the garment.

3. If you are binding a neckline, sew the right shoulder seam and leave the left shoulder seam unstitched. You cannot use a binder attachment to apply binding to a continuous edge or to a circle.

4. Apply the binding until it goes a bit past the end, then trim the binding to line up to the shoulder edges.

5. Finally, close the remaining shoulder seam and binding.

When binding a continuous edge on a cardigan, leave a few inches of the left side seam open so you can start and end the binding. To bind sleeveless garments, leave the side seam open. Bind sleeve hems before closing the sleeve. When binding the ends at the finished garment hem, cut the binding ½ in. to 1 in. longer than the garment so you can turn back the edges to line up with the hemline and topstitch in place.

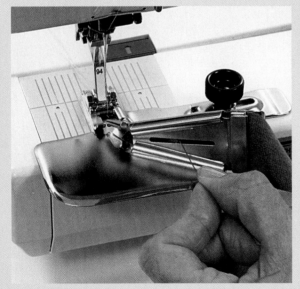

When using a binder attachment, feed the binding so the wrong side of the fabric is facing you as you slide the fabric through.

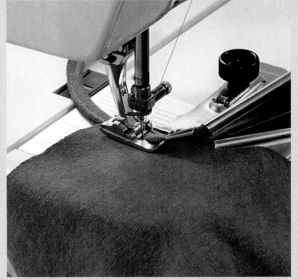

Sew the binding using either a straight stitch or a narrow zigzag stitch, going a bit past the end, then trim the binding to line up with the shoulder edge.

You can use a binder attachment to add bindings to garments in a variety of ways.

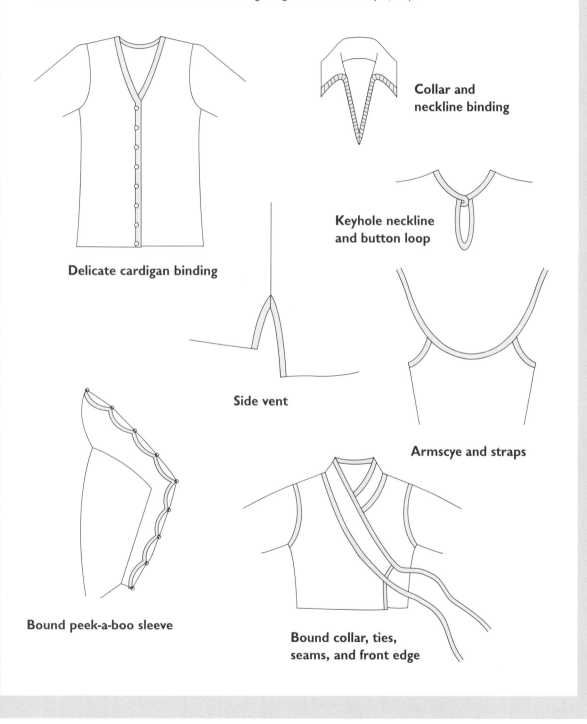

Collar and neckline binding

Keyhole neckline and button loop

Delicate cardigan binding

Side vent

Armscye and straps

Bound peek-a-boo sleeve

Bound collar, ties, seams, and front edge

TIP

If a pattern does not call for binding but you would like to add it anyway, cut away the seam allowance of the edge you plan to bind. This way the outer edge of the bound neckline will fall along the original seamline.

Binding

Bindings enclose the neckline and edges and add stability to the edges while allowing for some stretch. You can use binding as an alternative to facings. The binding fabric may be the same as the fashion fabric or it may be contrasting, but it must have some stretch. Select lightweight ribbing, jersey, interlock, or knits with spandex for binding fabric.

There are many types of binding. French binding, also called double binding, can be adapted to various kinds of fabric and looks the same on both sides. Single-layer binding is less bulky than French binding because it is not folded under on the inside of the garment. Single-layer binding is good for necklines, hems, and bulky knits such as synthetic fleece. Narrow single-layer bindings look wonderful on delicate and sheer knits. The easiest way to attach a narrow single-layer binding that has a turned-under edge on the outside and inside of a garment is with a binder attachment (see the sidebar on pp. 52-53).

Binding with a finished width of ½ in. is a good size to use on a variety of knitted fabrics, although you can adjust the width to suit your taste and the type of fabric you are using. Bindings that are narrower than ½ in. work well on thin and lightweight fabrics, but wide bindings should be less than 1 in. because they don't follow curves as well and are more difficult to apply.

While woven bindings must be cut on the bias, it is unnecessary for knits because weft knits stretch on the crossgrain just as much or more than bias wovens. Use knits on the bias only if you have a patterned fabric that creates a different or unusual effect when cut that way. Otherwise, crosswise stretch is more consistent and uses less fabric.

Applying single-layer binding Single-layer binding can be used on necklines, sleeves, and hems. To make a binding, cut the binding fabric four times the desired finished width. For example, for a ½-in.-wide binding, cut the fabric 2 in. wide and 2 in. to 3 in. longer than the seam being

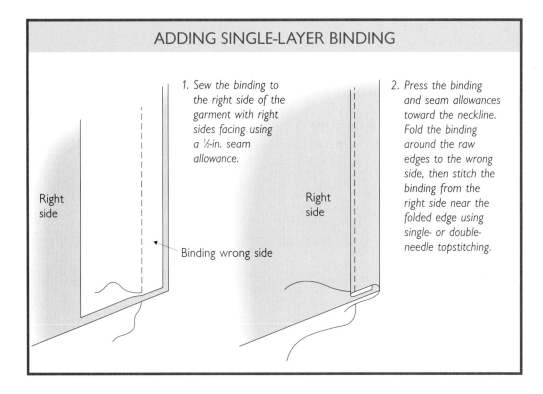

ADDING SINGLE-LAYER BINDING

1. Sew the binding to the right side of the garment with right sides facing using a ½-in. seam allowance.

Right side

Binding wrong side

2. Press the binding and seam allowances toward the neckline. Fold the binding around the raw edges to the wrong side, then stitch the binding from the right side near the folded edge using single- or double-needle topstitching.

Right side

finished. You may finish one long edge of the binding with a machine overlock stitch or a serger stitch. Otherwise, trim away the excess binding after topstitching.

If you are going to apply the binding to a circular edge such as a neckline, hem, or sleeve, leave one garment seam open so the binding can be applied flat. To bind a hem, sew one side seam of the garment, and apply the binding to the right side before sewing the second side seam. You can also use this method for sleeve hems.

1. *To apply binding to a neckline, sew one shoulder seam, then matching raw edges, sew the right side of the binding to the right side of the neckline using a ½-in. seam allowance (see the illustration on the facing page). Stretch the binding slightly at inside curves, and ease the binding slightly at outside curves.*
2. *Finger-press the binding toward the seam allowance, and trim away excess binding at the ends.*
3. *Next, stitch the remaining shoulder seam, including the binding.*
4. *Fold the binding around the raw edges to the wrong side, then pin in the well of the seam on the right side to hold it in place.*
5. *Stitch the binding near the folded edge using single- or double-needle topstitching.*

Applying French binding French binding is good to use when you can see the inside of the garment, such as on vests, cardigans, and outerwear, or anytime you want a sturdy finish. It is especially important to use lightweight fabric for this binding because the double layer must wrap around the garment edge. You can check the thickness by folding the binding fabric in half, pinning it to the fashion fabric ½ in. from the edge with raw edges aligned, and wrapping the binding around to enclose the edge.

To make the binding, cut the fabric on the crosswise grain for maximum stretch, making it six times the desired width plus about ½ in. extra. The extra makes up for loss of width due to turning and stretching

around the cut edges and allows for some overlap at the topstitching. For a ½-in.-wide finished binding, cut the binding 3½ in. to 3⅝ in. wide and 2 in. to 3 in. longer than the edge you are binding.

Ideally, one continuous piece of fabric should be used to finish even the longest seam, but doing this is unlikely on long edges. Piecing is inevitable. You should

When piecing fabric for a binding, piece plain knits diagonally and ribbed knits following a rib.

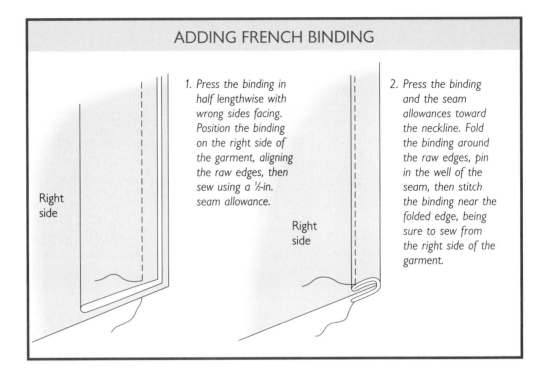

ADDING FRENCH BINDING

Right side

1. Press the binding in half lengthwise with wrong sides facing. Position the binding on the right side of the garment, aligning the raw edges, then sew using a ½-in. seam allowance.

Right side

2. Press the binding and the seam allowances toward the neckline. Fold the binding around the raw edges, pin in the well of the seam, then stitch the binding near the folded edge, being sure to sew from the right side of the garment.

piece ribbed binding following a rib, but piece plain knits diagonally.

To apply binding to a circular edge, such as a neckline or sleeve, or to a continuous edge around a cardigan front or vest, leave one garment seam open so the binding can be applied flat. On a neckline, leave one shoulder seam open, and on a cardigan or vest, leave one side seam open.

1. *To bind a neckline, press the binding in half lengthwise with wrong sides together.*
2. *Position the binding on the neckline, aligning the raw edges of the binding and the neckline on the right side of the garment, then sew using a ½-in. seam allowance (see the illustration above).*
3. *Finger-press the binding toward the seam allowance.*
4. *Next, cut away the excess binding length, and trim the seam allowances near the binding ends and at intersecting seams to reduce bulk.*
5. *Sew the remaining shoulder seam, including the binding.*

6. *Finally, fold the binding around the raw edge, pin it in the well of the seam, and stitch the binding near the folded edge. Be sure to sew from the right side of the garment.*

Ribbing

Using ribbing is an easy way to finish necklines and edges that need to stretch. T-shirts, sweatshirts, and sweaterknits typically have ribbed trim, but you can also use ribbing as a trim on woven garments.

Cutting neckline ribbing Part of the fun of sewing is creating your own original, copying something you love wearing, or just changing the size and shape of a neckline to suit your preferences. Here is a guide for cutting ribbing when you don't have a pattern. It's easier than you think.

To cut the ribbing length, measure the neck opening along the stitching line. Divide this measurement by two-thirds, and add two seam allowances. When adding ribbing to woven garments or knits that do not stretch, such as raschel knits, cut the ribbing length to equal three-quarters the size of the neckline plus two seam allowances.

If ribbing will be folded over when it is applied, cut the width to be twice the desired width plus two seam allowances. You can use ¼-in. seam allowances if the ribbing and the body fabric are fine knits and don't unravel easily. On bulky knits and knits that do unravel easily, use ½-in. seam allowances, and trim away the excess during or after attaching the ribbing. For a folded trim 1 in. wide using a ½-in. seam allowance, cut the ribbing 3 in. wide.

Ribbing with a finished edge, such as the ribbed trim on sweaterbodies and packaged ribbing, can be applied using a single thickness. In this case, cut the width of the ribbing to equal the desired width plus one seam allowance. For a finished trim 1 in. wide using a ½-in. seam allowance, cut 1½-in.-wide ribbing.

Sewing and attaching the ribbing

Dividing the ribbing and neckline into fourths is the key to distributing the ribbing, resulting in a smooth, even width around the neckline.

1. *With right sides together, use a straight stitch on a sewing machine or use a serger to sew the ends of the ribbing together to form a circle.*
2. *Finger-press the seam open, or clip the seam allowance to the stitching at the center fold and finger-press the seam allowance in opposite directions to reduce bulk. If you use a serger stitch, finger-press the seam allowance in opposite directions without clipping the seam (see the illustration on p. 58).*
3. *With wrong sides together, fold the ribbing in half lengthwise, then machine-baste the raw edges together, staying close to the edges. Stretch the ribbing as you baste.*
4. *For a neckline, divide the ribbing and the neckline into fourths, and mark the divisions using a marker or pins. To be accurate, stretch the ribbing when dividing it.*

TIP

An nonmathematical way to decide the length of a ribbed trim is to first cut it the desired width going all the way across the fabric. Fold the ribbing in half lengthwise, and run it along the edge of the neckline that you are finishing, starting at a shoulder seam and stretching the ribbing as you go. Following the curve of the neckline, stretch the cut edge as much as possible without straining it to allow the folded edge, which will be closest to the neck, to lie flat when you wear the garment.

The center front and center back are the halfway points, but the shoulder seams are rarely the midpoints between the front and back unless the garment has the same neckline front and back.

5. *Place the ribbing seam at the center back of the neckline, then pin the ribbing to the neckline with right sides facing, matching the quarter divisions and raw edges (see the illustration on p. 58).*
6. *With the ribbing on top, sew using a stretch stitch on a sewing machine or using a serger.*

Ribbing also may be used as a sleeve finish. In this case, cut the ribbing length equal to the wrist measurement plus two seam allowances, and cut the ribbing width equal to twice the desired width plus two seam allowances. A standard finished cuff and waist finish is about 2½ in. wide, but you can vary the width to suit the proportions of your garment and choice of fabric. For a 2½-in.-wide cuff with ½-in. seam allowances, cut the trim 6 in. wide. Sew following the directions for finishing the neckline, including dividing the trim and the sleeve into quarters.

In addition to necklines and sleeves, you can add ribbing to the lower edge of a garment. First measure the lower edge, then cut the length of the ribbing equal to two-thirds this measurement plus two seam allowances. You could also cut it to a

TIP

A garment and ribbing must have the same seam allowance, so if the garment has a ⅝-in. seam allowance the ribbing must also have a ⅝-in. seam allowance.

TIP

To attach the ribbing flat rather than in the round, follow the same sewing sequence as for attaching binding on pp. 54-55.

CUTTING AND APPLYING RIBBING TO A NECKLINE

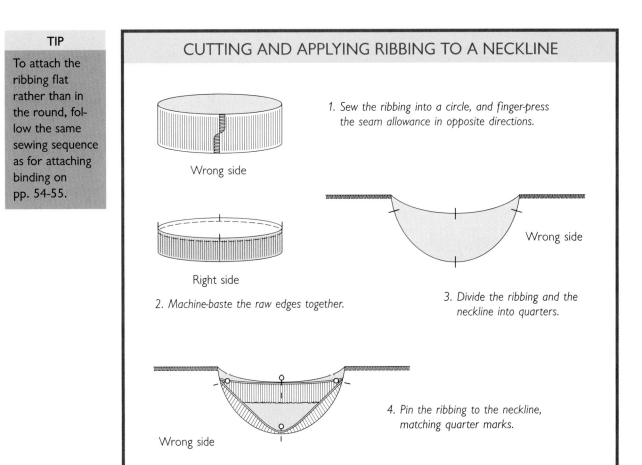

Wrong side

1. *Sew the ribbing into a circle, and finger-press the seam allowance in opposite directions.*

Right side

2. *Machine-baste the raw edges together.*

Wrong side

3. *Divide the ribbing and the neckline into quarters.*

Wrong side

4. *Pin the ribbing to the neckline, matching quarter marks.*

length that fits comfortably around your body plus two seam allowances. Cut the ribbing width to twice the desired width of the finished trim plus two seam allowances. Sew following the directions for finishing the neckline, placing the ribbing seam at the left side seam.

Attaching ribbing to a V-neckline   A V-neckline can be in the front, the back, or both. Attaching ribbing to necklines that have corners, such as V-necklines, square necklines, and sweetheart necklines, is easy to do if you miter the corners after attaching the ribbing.

1. *Using a fabric marker or thread, mark the garment's center front or back at the neckline so the V will be perfectly centered.*

Also mark the seamline for about 2 in. on either side of the center, and staystitch the corner in the seam allowance ⅛ in. from the seamline. Clip the corner to the staystitching (see the illustration on the facing page).

TIP

Because ribbed fabrics and trims have so many variables, it is always a good idea to compare the length of the ribbing to the part of the garment it finishes as well as the body part it covers. Do this before sewing the ribbing in place. Always make sure turtlenecks and crewnecks fit over the wearer's head and that cuffs and waistbands are close enough to the body without being too tight.

2. *Measure, cut, and sew the neck ribbing in the same manner as for round necklines. Sew the ribbing in place, since this will make mitering the V much easier.*

3. *Next, fold the neckline ribbing along the center with right sides facing, and make a miter that should be approximately 45 degrees.*

4. *Finally, pin or baste, then sew from the folded edge to the point of the neckline. It is only necessary to trim the excess seam at the miter if the knit is very bulky.*

Neckline Finishes for Stable Knits

Replacing shaped facings with straight facings or purchased single-fold bias tape results in a simple and lightweight edge. Straight facings and bias tape are often interchangeable—both accomplish a simple, narrow edge finish that is turned to the inside and topstitched in place. Self-

fabric straight facings look better than bias tape, are always the perfect match, and wear at the same rate as the garment. On the other hand, purchased bias tape is useful when using self-fabric makes the edge too bulky. Try using these methods on single knits and matte jersey when other finishes don't work.

Straight facings   When finishing the edges of knits with little to moderate stretch, you can use strips of the fashion fabric instead of shaped facings. Straight facings are crosswise strips of the fashion fabric or binding that are turned completely to the inside of the garment and then topstitched from the right side. They do not need interfacing. The binding fabric must have enough stretch to conform to the neckline or armhole shape, but some knits, such as those with spandex, may have too

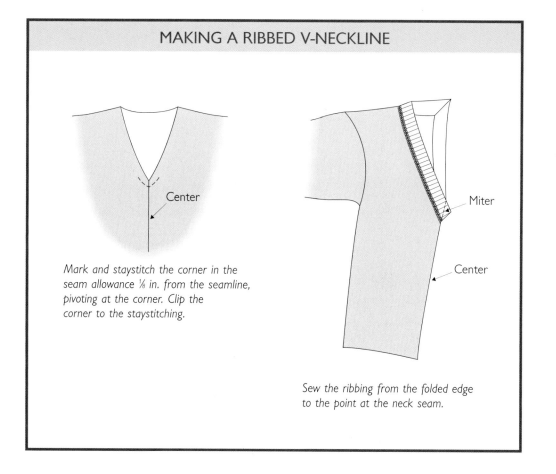

MAKING A RIBBED V-NECKLINE

Mark and staystitch the corner in the seam allowance ⅛ in. from the seamline, pivoting at the corner. Clip the corner to the staystitching.

Center

Miter

Center

Sew the ribbing from the folded edge to the point at the neck seam.

much stretch and are best finished using one of the swimsuit techniques.

1. To make straight facings, cut a crosswise strip of the garment fabric ¾ in. wide plus the width of the seam allowance. If the seam allowance is ¼ in. wide, cut the strip 1 in. wide.
2. Finish one edge using a medium zigzag stitch, an overlock stitch, or a stretch overlock stitch on a sewing machine. If using a serger, use a three-thread serger stitch.
3. Next, decide how long to cut the straight facing in one of two ways. You could cut the facing to equal three-quarters the length of the edge plus ½ in. to sew it together. You could also run the facing strip along the edge you are finishing, lining up the raw edges and stretching the facing to follow the garment edge. To keep the edge from stretching out when you sew the facing or wear the garment, the finished edge of the facing should be stretched to follow the garment's curves. Stretch the trim as much as possible without straining the garment edge.
4. Pin the facing to the right side of the neckline or armhole opening with right sides facing and the raw edges aligned. Be sure to place the facing seam at an inconspicuous place, such as the underarm seam of the armhole or the center back seam on the neckline.
5. After pinning, cut the facing trim to the size of the neckline plus ¼-in. seam allowances at each end for sewing.
6. To make the straight facing easier to sew in place, first sew the ends to form a circle.
7. Starting at the facing seam, stitch the seam with a straight stitch or narrow zigzag. If you are using a ⅝-in. seam allowance, trim the seam allowance to ¼ in. after sewing the seam. Clip the seam allowances at the curves, then press the straight facing and the seam allowances toward the neckline.
8. Turn the facing to the inside of the garment, pin, and topstitch with the right side of the garment opening facing up. Start sewing at the least conspicuous garment seam, such as the underarm or shoulder seam, and sew a few stitches past the start, locking in the stitch by sewing in place.

Stretch the facing trim as much as possible without straining the outside edge and pin in place, then cut the trim to size allowing ¼ in. at each end.

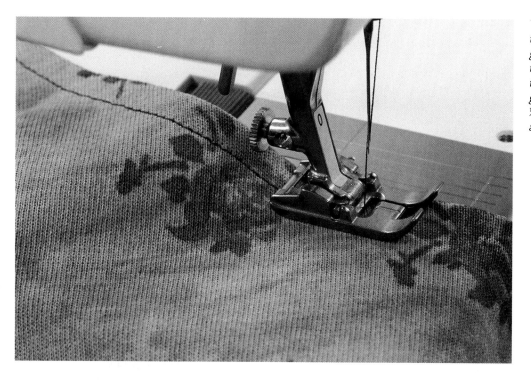

Turn the facing to the inside of the garment, pin, and topstitch with the right side of the garment up using a ¼-in. to ⅜-in. seam allowance.

Single-fold bias tape Single-fold bias tape creates a stable garment edge that is not meant to stretch. It is a good choice for finishing necklines and edges on knits that are stable or have a small amount of stretch, but it's a bad choice for knits with two-way stretch or spandex because it is easy to either stretch out the neckline or to control it to excess. Using such a stable neckline finish defeats the purpose of using fabric with lots of stretch. Do not staystitch the neckline when using this technique even if the pattern directions call for it— you will stretch the neckline out of shape.

1. *To use single-fold bias tape, unfold one edge of the tape and pin it to the neckline edge with right sides facing and the raw edges even. If there is a neck opening, extend the ends of the binding ½ in. beyond the opening. If the opening is circular, such as a neckline or armhole edge, fold back ¼ in. at one end of the binding and start pinning, placing the folded edge either next to the underarm seam on the armhole or next to the shoulder seam on the neckline.*

TIP

Single-fold bias tape is overused in the directions given by some pattern companies. You should use it as the neckline and edge finish of last resort when other finishes don't work.

At the other end, lap the cut edge on top of the folded-back edge so the ends are even (see the top photo on p. 62). If the neckline has a neck opening, press back the raw edges at both ends of the binding so that the folded ends line up with the neck opening or zipper teeth (see the bottom photo on p. 62).
2. *Stitch using a ⅜-in. seam allowance on the unfolded crease line of the binding, then trim the seam allowance to ¼ in. so that it doesn't show past the folded binding edge.*
3. *Fold the bias tape over the seam allowance to the inside of the garment along the seamline, then press the edge with the bias facing up.*

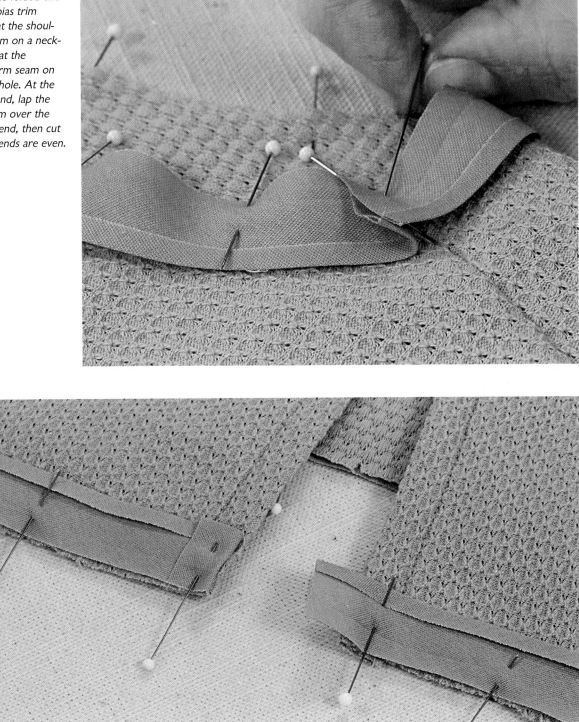

Place the folded end of the bias trim either at the shoulder seam on a neckline or at the underarm seam on an armhole. At the other end, lap the bias trim over the folded end, then cut so the ends are even.

If the neckline has an opening, cut the trim so that it extends ½ in. beyond the opening, then press back the raw edges at both ends so that the folded ends line up with the opening or with the zipper fold.

4. *Next, examine the width of the binding to determine the seam allowance that will place the stitching close to the inner folded binding edge. Check for narrow areas in the binding so you don't go beyond the folded edge when you topstitch. The stitching should be about ⅜ in. away from the neckline edge.*
5. *Place pins perpendicular to the neckline edge to allow easy removal, then topstitch with the right side of the garment facing up, starting at the neckline opening or the binding overlap.*
6. *Finally, secure the folded ends of the bias tape using a topstitch or a slipstitch.*

ADDING ELASTIC WAISTBANDS

Elasticized waistlines are comfortable, practical, and easy to do. The elastic may be inserted into a casing or stitched in place. The advantage to inserting the elastic into a casing is that you can adjust the elastic for a perfect fit as you sew. Stitched-in elastic permanently positions the elastic in the waistband and may be topstitched several different ways. Draw-cord elastic, which is applied this way, has the benefit of having additional room for adjustment because of this built-in draw cord.

Visible Elastic Waistbands

Using a casing with either single or multiple rows of elastic are easy ways to finish a comfortable waistband on garments that have a considerable amount of ease. Most patterns with elastic waistbands use one of these methods.

Making a casing using a single row of elastic When making a casing, the width should equal the width of the elastic plus ½ in., which allows room for stitching the casing in place. Be sure to choose firm, nonroll elastic. When sewing knits, the casing edge is not turned under as would be necessary when using wovens.

1. *Begin by folding down the casing at the waist edge and stitching a channel that is ⅛ in. wider than the width of the elastic. Start and end near the center back seam, leaving a 2-in. opening. If there is no*

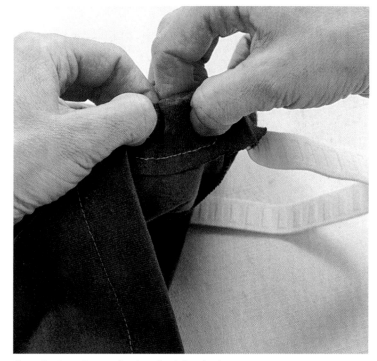

For a basic casing application, feed the elastic through the casing using a safety pin.

Pull both ends of the elastic out of the casing far enough to easily overlap them, then sew the ends.

Clipping to the vertical seam along the casing fold line allows you to fold back the seam allowances on both sides of the seam opening and stitch them in place, then double-stitch or overlock the garment seams together below the facing.

center back seam, leave an opening at one of the side seams.

2. Measure the elastic around your waist, and cut it 1 in. longer than what feels comfortable. How tightly you stretch the elastic depends on your comfort level and on the firmness of the elastic.

3. Next, feed the elastic through the casing using a large safety pin. Overlap the elastic ends, and stitch using a straight stitch or a zigzag stitch.

4. Stretch the waistline so that the elastic pops into the casing, then finish sewing the casing seam.

Making a casing using multiple rows of elastic   Multiple rows of narrow elastic may be substituted for a single row of wide elastic without changing the pattern or the size of the casing as long as you choose an elastic size that is compatible with the size of the casing. To use multiple rows of elastic, the size of each casing or the space between each row of stitching should be ⅛ in. wider than the elastic. For example, to use ½-in.-wide elastic, the rows of stitching should be ⅝ in. apart. To use ⅜-in.-wide elastic, the rows of stitching should be ½ in. apart.

Here are some practical substitutes. If a pattern calls for one row of 1-in.-wide elastic, you may easily substitute two rows of ⅜-in.-wide elastic by stitching two parallel rows of stitching ½ in. apart, starting ½ in. from the top fold. If a pattern calls for one row of 1½-in.-wide elastic, you can substitute three rows of ⅜-in.-wide elastic by sewing three parallel rows of topstitching ½ in. apart. If a pattern calls for one row of 2-in.-wide elastic, you can substitute four rows of ⅜-in. elastic by sewing four parallel rows of topstitching ½ in. apart.

1. To use multiple rows, start by stitching the vertical garment seams, leaving the back side of the casing open at the center back seam so that you can feed the elastic through. This is done by leaving the casing seam open starting a tiny amount past the casing foldline and ending ½ in. from the

Tie multiple elastics together at one end to prevent the ends from slipping into the casing, then insert each elastic into the casing simultaneously using safety pins.

cut edge. If there is no back seam, leave an opening at one of the side seams.

2. Clip the vertical seam allowance along the casing foldline.

3. Next, fold back the seam allowances on either side of the opening, and stitch them in place. If you like, finish the casing edge with a machine or serger overlock stitch.

4. Fold the casing to the wrong side and pin, then stitch parallel rows of stitches, starting with the row closest to the fold. The number of rows and the distance apart depends on the pattern you are using.

5. Cut the elastic to fit the waist plus 1 in., then tie the two, three, or four elastic ends together at one end to prevent the ends from slipping into the casings prematurely. Using a safety pin on each end, insert the elastics into their casings. Work the elastic through each casing simultaneously.

6. Once the elastics are in their casings, untie them, then overlap the ends and pin them to form circles. After making sure the elastics are not twisted, sew them together. The casing opening may be slipstitched closed or left alone since the seam allowance is stitched in place.

Casing elastic may be stitched to the vertical seams to permanently distribute the ease. To do this, try on the garment and adjust the side seams so they are visually centered when looking at the body sideways. Pin to hold them in place, then remove the garment. Stitch in the well of the seam from the right side along the side,

TIP

When changing the elastic application recommended on a pattern, it is safer to switch from stitching it in to using a casing than it is to switch from using a casing to stitching it in. When stitching in elastic, variables in the stretch of the elastic compared with the amount of ease in the garment and in the resilience of the fashion fabric affect the final size of the waistband. Stitching through elastic changes its length, and the more times you stitch through the elastic the more you may increase its size. The exception where this wouldn't happen is when sewing a very close-fitting garment with little ease such as on spandex fabrics.

center front, and center back seams, being sure that the elastic is equally distributed.

Making a stitched-in-place casing

Stitched-in elastic permanently positions the elastic to the waistband. It is best suited for waistlines with little to moderate ease because the elastic must be stretched to the size of the waistline in order to sew it in place. For this application, the width of the casing is equal to the width of the elastic.

1. Start by overlapping the ends of the elastic and sewing to form a circle.
2. Divide the elastic and the waistline into quarters.
3. Next, pin the elastic to the wrong side of the casing, lining up the edge of the elastic to the raw edge of the casing and matching quarter marks.
4. Serge or use a zigzag that is 2mm wide and long to sew the elastic to the casing, stretching just enough to make the fabric lie flat.

For an invisible waistband, form a circle with the elastic by butting the ends of the elastic and sewing back and forth using a triple zigzag or a wide zigzag.

5. Fold the casing to the wrong side to cover the elastic.
6. If you are using wide elastic, topstitch the waistband using one or multiple rows of stitching. To do this, first stitch the casing in place at each seam by sewing in the well of the seam from the right side of the garment.

Invisible Elastic Waistbands

There are several ways to apply elastic to the waist area that avoid sewing a casing and visible stitching. The resulting waist treatments look smooth and do not have the obviously elasticized waist that you see on sporty clothes and pull-on styles, so they are especially suitable for more dressed-up styles and fabrics. Invisible elasticized waist treatments are only appropriate for styles that have a smooth fit, have very little ease at the waist, and use fabrics with moderate stretch or better.

The first method, which is suitable for thin fabrics, retains a casing but eliminates topstitching. The second and third applications reduce bulk and are especially good to use on pile fabrics such as velvet, but they are also appropriate for all knitted fabrics when you want to avoid the elastic-casing look but retain the elastic-casing comfort. In these methods, the elastic acts as a waist facing and is exposed on the inside of the garment. Eliminating the back side of the casing means pile fabrics will not stick to a blouse or top that is tucked into the waistline.

Preparing the elastic and garment
For all three methods, choose firm, nonroll elastic in the width required by the pattern, then prepare the elastic and garment.

1. Start by cutting elastic to fit comfortably around your waist. A good size to use is 1 in. to 2 in. smaller than the waist measurement since the elastic will stretch a bit when sewn in place. If your pattern calls for stitched-in-place elastic, the size dictated in the directions minus seam allowances also works.

2. Form a circle with the elastic by butting the ends together and stitching back and forth using a wide zigzag or a three-step zigzag. This produces a firm and flat seam.
3. Finally, divide the elastic and the garment waistline into quarters, and mark using a fabric marker.

Making an invisible elastic casing   If your fabric is not bulky, you may still create an invisible casing by positioning the elastic inside a casing but stitching the elastic to the casing allowance only. This method is nice to use on basic knits as well as matte jersey, slinky knits, and knits with spandex. Eliminating the topstitching makes the casing invisible.

Using a pattern that has a waist casing and without making any changes to the pattern, sew the elastic as follows.

1. Position and pin the elastic to the wrong side of the waist casing, matching quarter marks.
2. Using a medium zigzag stitch or a serger, sew the outermost edge with the elastic on top, being sure not to cut the elastic when using the serger (see the photo below).

For an invisible elastic casing, stretch the elastic just enough to fit the fabric edge and sew using a medium zigzag stitch or using a three-thread serger stitch.

Sew a second zigzag along the inner edge of the elastic.

3. Sew a second zigzag stitch along the inner edge of the elastic as shown in the photo above.
4. Turn the elastic and casing to the inside of the garment, and secure the casing to the outer garment by sewing in the well of each vertical seam from the outside.

Making an overlapped elastic facing

A simple way to install the elastic is to leave the pattern unchanged, position the elastic next to the foldline on the outside of the casing, and trim away most of the casing allowance after stitching the elastic in place. Sewing the elastic so that the side lines up with the top edge of the garment gives the flattest results. The only possible disadvantage is that the elastic is not set back from the top edge, so you might see the edge of the elastic peeking out at the upper edge.

1. Begin by positioning and pinning the elastic to the right side of the garment on top of the casing, being sure to match the quarter marks. Line up one edge of the elastic to the casing foldline. The other edge of the elastic should be near the cut edge of the casing.
2. If the garment fabric has a pile or is velvet, first machine-baste the edge of the elastic to prevent shifting. Sew the permanent seam along the elastic edge nearest the foldline, using a medium zigzag stitch 2mm wide and 2mm long. When sewing, the left swing of the needle should pierce the edge of the elastic or swing slightly over the elastic edge.
3. Trim away the casing fabric next to the zigzag stitch, leaving a ¼-in. seam. Turn the elastic to the inside of the garment, and stitch in place to all the garment's vertical seams. To sew by machine, sew from the right side of the garment in the well of each vertical seam. To sew by hand, tack the elastic to each vertical seam allowance on the inside of the garment.

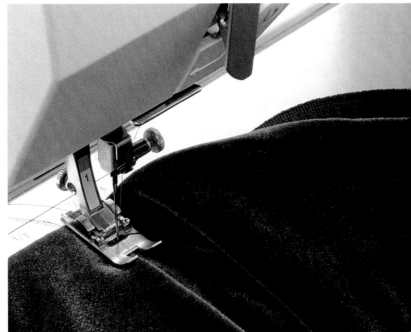

For an elastic facing, permanently sew the elastic to the waist seam using a ¼-in. seam allowance and a medium zigzag or a serger. When using this application on pile fabrics, machine-baste the elastic in place first.

Turn the elastic to the inside of the garment, and stitch in place at all vertical seams. Topstitch from the right side of the garment on top of the existing seam.

Making an elastic facing With this method, fashion fabric covers the upper edge of the elastic. Before preparing the elastic and garment, you must first adapt the pattern by changing the waist cutting line. Do this by finding the casing foldline on the pattern and adding a ⅝-in. seam allowance to mark the new waist cutting line. If the pattern does not show a foldline but simply states how much has been allowed for the casing, change that allowance to ⅝ in. and use that as the cutting line.

1. *To install the elastic, line up and pin one side of the elastic with the raw edge of the waist seam with right sides facing and matching quarter marks. Line up the fabric to the elastic so that the fabric extends just a bit past the elastic edge. This is so you can keep track of the fabric layer during sewing.*

2. *If you are using a pile fabric, which has a tendency to shift as you sew, machine-baste the elastic to the waist seam using a long straight stitch. Baste with the elastic on top, stretching the elastic only enough to smooth the garment fabric underneath and avoid tucks. Be sure to stop frequently with the needle down, and adjust the outer edge of the fabric just before it reaches the presser foot.*

3. *Using a medium zigzag stitch or a serger, permanently sew the seam using a ¼-in. seam allowance. Be sure to avoid cutting the elastic.*

4. *Turn the elastic to the inside of the garment, and stitch in place at all vertical seams. Topstitch from the right side, sewing right on top of the existing seams. When you do this, about ⅜ in. of the garment fabric will be turned to the inside of the garment, covering the elastic near the upper edge of the waistline.*

4 Further Techniques and Finishing Touches

Here you will find ways to make your knitted garments more successful while adding those perfect finishing touches that can make a project work. These are methods that may not be included in your pattern instructions but are easy to do for a custom look and professional finish. You will learn how to stabilize shoulder seams, add zippers and buttonholes that won't stretch out of shape, add pockets both subtle and decorative, as well has how to make a beautiful color-blocked garment.

STABILIZING SHOULDER SEAMS

Some seams need to be stabilized because they are more likely to stretch out of shape. Purchased bias tricot, such as Seams Great, or clear elastic stabilize a seam without removing all the stretch. To use these, cut the tricot or elastic the same length as the seam. If you choose to use ⅜-in.-wide bias tricot, center the tricot trim along the stitching line of the seam, then sew using a machine or serger overlock stitch or using double-stitched seams.

Shoulder seams can be stabilized with bias tricot trim. To do so, center ⅜-in.-wide bias tricot trim over the seamline, then sew the seam.

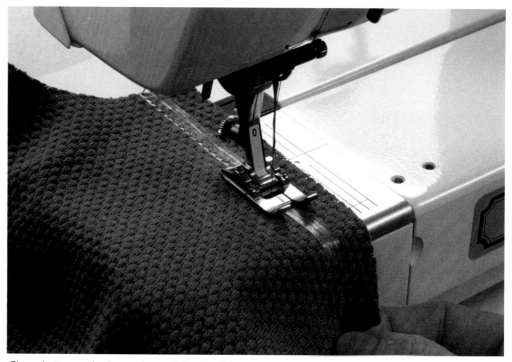

Clear elastic can also be used to stabilize shoulder seams. Position most of the elastic in the seam allowance, and catch the edge of the elastic as you sew the seam.

If you want to use clear elastic, select one that is ¼ in. or ⅜ in. wide. Position most of the elastic on the seam allowance, then stitch the seam with the elastic on top of the fabric and without stretching it. Be sure to catch the edge of the elastic as you sew the seam. Next, sew the seam and the elastic a second time using an appropriate seam finish for your fabric.

If you use a serger instead of a sewing machine, you can sew the seam, the elastic, and the edge finish in one step. When using a serger, clear elastic tends to stick and not feed back easily at the start of a seam. You can overcome this by cutting the elastic 2 in. longer than the seam. This way you can start sewing with the elastic extending behind the presser foot and use the end of the elastic as a handle when you start sewing the seam.

If your fashion fabric is not too thick, you can use a lengthwise strip of the fashion fabric to stabilize the shoulder area instead of bias tricot or elastic. This works with all knits that are thin and have lengthwise stability. The advantage is that you already own the fabric and the stabilizer will match perfectly. To use this method, line up the raw edges and sew the seam, catching the lengthwise strip.

Another option is to use a lengthwise strip of fusible tricot interfacing. To do this, cut the tricot interfacing lengthwise so it

---

TIP

On a heavy fabric such as chenille, position 1¼-in.-wide tricot along the fabric edge so that it curls up and away from the seam, then stitch using a ⅜-in. seam allowance. Finger-press both tricot edges toward the seam allowance, and stitch again about ¼ in. away or serge. Doing this places two layers of tricot in the seam allowance and increases the stability of the seam.

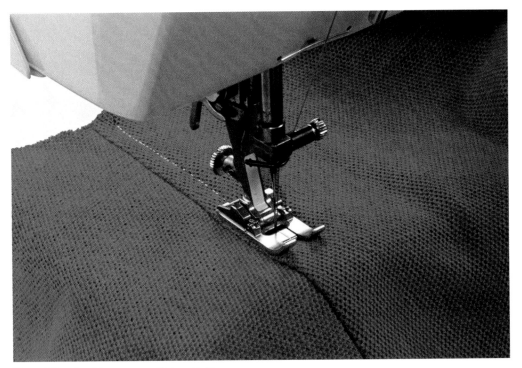

To stabilize shoulder seams with topstitching, sew then press seams to one side. Topstitch with the right side of the garment facing up. The width of the topstitched seam can be any amount less than the width of the garment seam.

has minimum stretch and is ¼ in. wider than the seam allowance. Line up the raw edges, and fuse it to the wrong side of either the front or back shoulder seam, then sew the front to the back.

You may also stabilize seams by top-stitching after the seams are sewn. To use this technique, which works best on stable knits, press the seams to one side or open, then topstitch with the right side of the garment facing up. Sew a distance from the seam that is narrower than the seam allowance. For variety you can use a medium zigzag stitch or a double-needle straight stitch to topstitch the seams.

INSERTING ZIPPERS

Separating zippers are attractive and practical on knit garments, particularly thick knits such as fleece and pile fabrics, because button closures must overlap and overlapped front edges can get thick. When a regular zipper is necessary, invisible zippers are the best choice because they are compatible with all types of fabrics and do not call attention to the zipper closure.

There are many ways to install zippers. I have two favorite ways for inserting separating zippers on knit garments. The first method avoids topstitching and lets you focus on the zipper, and the second method uses topstitching but not to sew the actual zipper in place. Any topstitching on solid-colored fleece really stands out, sometimes more than the zipper, so it must be perfect.

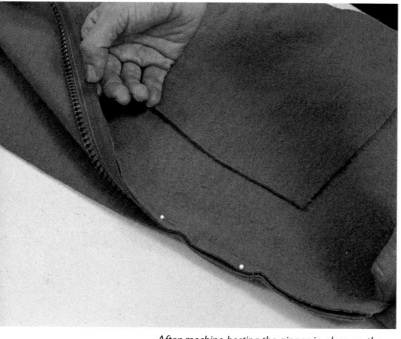

After machine-basting the zipper in place on the seam, pin the facing to the garment with right sides together, and sew only the zipper seam using a zipper foot. Sew the permanent stitch directly on top of the basting stitch.

Separating Zipper without Topstitching

If your garment has front facings, you can eliminate topstitching by using this method.

1. *Start by separating the zipper, then pin and machine-baste one side of the zipper to the front edge of the garment with right sides together and the teeth along the seamline.*
2. *Temporarily close the zipper, and pin the top and bottom of the remaining side to the other half of the garment, aligning the upper and lower edges.*
3. *Next, separate the zipper, and finish pinning and basting the second side. Close the zipper to check the placement.*
4. *With right sides together, pin the facing to the garment. Using a zipper foot, sew the zipper seam only over the basting stitch. The seam that attaches the facing also permanently attaches the zipper.*
5. *Finally, sew the neck edge of the facing using a standard foot.*

AVOID STRETCHING WHEN PINNING A ZIPPER

It is very important not to stretch the front edge of a garment as you pin and sew a zipper, which is especially easy when a zipper is longer than you need.

If your zipper is longer than the opening, compare it with the paper pattern, matching the lower edge of the zipper to the finished hemline or bottom placement mark on the pattern. Align the zipper to the front placement line or edge, and mark the top edge of the pattern on the zipper using a fabric marker. If the zipper installation continues on to the collar, pin the collar pattern to the front edge of the neckline, matching seams, then mark where the zipper should end on the zipper tape. You will be able to do a better job pinning on a table than on your lap. Always pin both ends of the zipper before pinning the middle so that you are forced to ease in any stretching that may have occurred at the front edge.

Once a zipper is pinned, machine-baste it in place with the zipper on top, stopping frequently to adjust the garment edge underneath the zipper tape. Help the zipper and the fabric stay aligned as they feed in front of the presser foot by squeezing the zipper and the fabric flat against the machine surface.

Topstitched Separating Zipper with No Facing

My favorite way to topstitch a separating zipper allows you to use a standard presser foot, which gives you a better-quality stitch. The other reason the topstitching looks better is that it is stitched down on the seam allowance that holds the zipper, rather than being stitched on the zipper tape. I like this method because it is open to creative variations.

1. *With right sides together, pin and machine-baste the separating zipper to the seam allowance using a zipper foot, aligning the zipper teeth to the seamline.*
2. *Close the zipper and check its placement, then permanently sew the zipper to the seam allowance only, sewing next to the zipper teeth.*
3. *Before topstitching, sew a second row of stitching along the outer edges of the zipper tape. Sewing with a standard presser foot and using a medium zigzag stitch set at 2mm to 3mm wide and long will finish the*

edge of the fabric and hold the edge of the zipper in place. This will also keep the zipper tape flat.
4. *Fold the front edge back next to the zipper teeth along the stitching line, then pin in place on the right side of the garment.*
5. *To topstitch, switch to a standard presser foot and sew approximately ½ in. away from the front fold, using a straight stitch or any of the decorative or utility stitches on your sewing machine that strikes your fancy.*

An easy way to customize this zipper application is to change the seam allowance at the zipper opening. Instead of using a ⅝-in. seam allowance, allow a 1-in., 2-in., or 3-in. seam allowance to create a bold front edge. The front edge remains the same, but the topstitching is done much farther away.

TIP

You always get a better stitch sewing with a standard foot than with a zipper foot because a standard foot has better contact with the fabric and better feeding action as you sew.

Before topstitching the zipper, sew a second row of stitching along the plain edge of the zipper tape. Sew using a standard zipper foot and a medium zigzag stitch 2mm to 3mm wide and long.

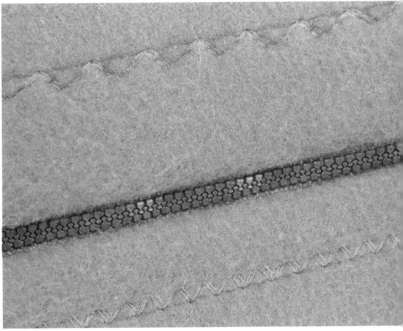

This sample shows two possible seam allowances that can be used at the zipper opening in place of a standard ⅝-in. seam allowance. Two different machine-utility stitches have been used as decorative topstitching to sew each seam allowance in place.

Invisible Zippers

My first thought when a pattern requires a zipper is to eliminate it if the fabric has enough stretch and the garment can be pulled over the body without stressing the seams. If a zipper is necessary, invisible zippers have no stitching on the outside of the garment, which makes them easy to sew neatly in place on a variety of fabrics, especially knits.

The key to the following technique is using a zipper that is longer than the zipper opening and basting before you sew. Purchase an invisible zipper 1 in. or more longer than the opening, or change the length of the opening to be shorter than the zipper. If you use a zipper the same size as the opening, it is not possible to sew the very bottom of the zipper in place because the zipper slider gets in the way. With a longer zipper you can place the excess length at the bottom, move the pull out of the way, and sew the bottom of the zipper with ease. Before beginning to install the zipper, sew the zipper seam below the zipper opening, stopping and backstitching at the zipper opening.

I always sew invisible zippers in two stages, first basting in place to position the zipper properly, then permanently stitching using an invisible zipper foot to get close to the zipper teeth. Basting first is especially useful when installing invisible zippers on knits because checking the placement as you sew is important to getting perfect results.

1. *Begin by placing the open zipper face down on the right side of the garment and pinning one side with the coil along the seamline and the excess length at the bottom. This places the slider below the opening and out of the way. Be sure to ease the seam to the zipper to allow for variations in the stretch of the fabric.*

TIP

You must allow for variations in a fabric's stretch that can affect a zipper seam. For example, you may install a zipper beautifully without stretching the seam, yet you'll have a bulging zipper when you put on the garment. That is because stretching the knitted fabric across contracts or pulls up the lengthwise seams. Easing more fabric into the zipper opening eliminates the bulge.

To install a separating zipper, pin one side of the zipper to the garment seam allowance with right sides together. Be sure to align the zipper teeth or coil to the seamline, place the excess length at the bottom of the zipper opening, and ease the seam to the zipper.

Finish pinning the zipper, again placing the coil along the seamline and being sure to ease the seam to the zipper.

2. Machine-baste one side of the zipper in place using a standard zipper foot and stopping at the bottom of the opening, not the bottom of the zipper. Keep the zipper teeth aligned to the seamline.

3. Next, close the zipper to determine the starting position for the second zipper tape on the remaining garment side. Pin the top and bottom of the tape to the seam allowance of the opening, then open the zipper and continue pinning the unstitched tape to the right side of the garment, positioning the coil along the seamline.

4. Machine-baste next to the zipper teeth using a standard zipper foot.

5. Close the zipper to be sure both sides are smooth, then try on the garment and check the seam. If the zipper bulges or ripples, rip out the basting and ease a bit more fabric into the zipper opening. Baste again and try on the garment.

6. Once the zipper is smooth, permanently sew the zipper. Machine-stitch the zipper in place using an invisible zipper foot and sewing

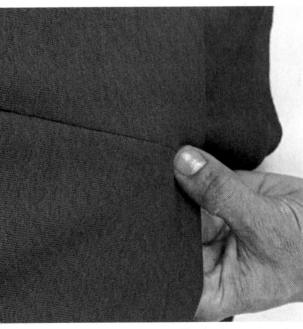

Close the zipper to see if both sides are smooth, then try on the garment to be sure the zipper is also smooth on the body. You may need to rebaste, increasing the amount of ease so the zipper doesn't bulge or ripple.

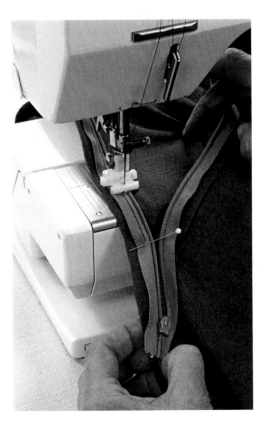

Permanently sew the zipper using an invisible zipper foot. The slider should be below the opening and out of the way.

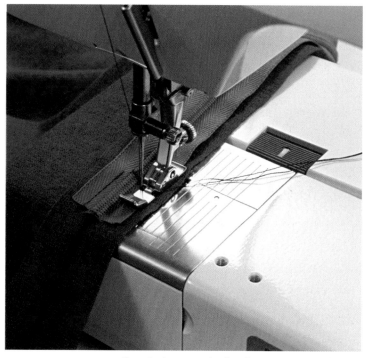

Sew the lower ends of each zipper tape to the garment seam allowances using a standard zipper foot.

close to the zipper teeth. Again, bring the slider below the zipper opening to do the permanent stitching, being sure to stitch to the bottom of the opening without going even one stitch past the bottom of the opening.

7. *To hold the bottom zipper ends down, stitch each tape end to a seam allowance only, not to the garment. Then open the zipper and stitch across the tops of the tapes at the neckline to keep the coil rolled back for easy sliding.*

MAKING BUTTONHOLES

Corded buttonholes are beautiful and practical on knitted fabrics. When making buttonholes on knits, they should be stabilized with gimp, buttonhole twist, or, better yet, elastic thread. The cording stabilizes a buttonhole to a certain size, while elastic thread creates an elastic buttonhole that is perfect for fabrics that stretch.

You can use elastic thread the same way you use gimp by stitching the buttonhole over the gimp without actually stitching through it. Most machine-buttonhole feet provide a way to anchor the gimp when you sew the buttonhole. After sewing the buttonholes, pull the ends of the elastic thread to the back of the garment using a crewel needle. Tie the ends together, reducing the length of the buttonhole to the desired size, then bury the threads between the layers of cloth, and cut away the excess.

Bulky or spongy knits may not feed through a machine well when you sew buttonholes. This causes the fabric to stay too long in the same place, stitches build up, and eventually the feeding stops altogether. Lengthening the stitch length helps the fabric feed more easily and improves the look of the buttonhole.

If altering the stitch length is not enough, using stabilizer on the bottom layer helps the fabric feed more easily. Try using

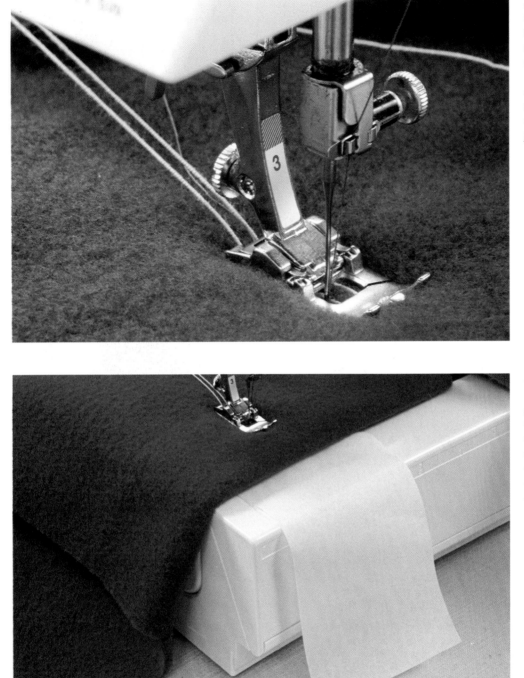

Sewing corded buttonholes using elastic thread allows you to create stable but elastic buttonholes. This buttonhole foot has a hook at the front to hold the cording while you sew.

Help spongy fabrics feed under the presser foot by using crisp paper or stabilizer under the garment. Increasing the stitch length also helps the fabric feed more easily.

water-soluble or tear-away stabilizer or just plain typing paper between the fabric and the feed dogs to help keep the fabric moving. If that is still not enough, using water-soluble stabilizer on top of and underneath the fabric will solve the problem. Both tear-away and typing paper leave bits of residue near the stitching, while water-soluble stabilizer simply dissolves when wet.

SEWING EASY POCKETS

Single-layer in-seam pockets and single-layer window pockets are attractive and practical pockets for wash-and-wear garments, but you will also appreciate how well they wear on things that you dry-clean.

Single-Layer In-Seam Pockets

Stitched-down, single-layer in-seam pockets stay in place and are half as bulky as standard in-seam pockets because you only use one pocket layer for each pocket. You can use them on tops, jackets, skirts, and pants in place of standard double-layer in-seam pockets.

1. *To make a single-layer in-seam pocket, start by stabilizing the pocket opening on the garment front using a ½-in.-wide lengthwise strip of fusible tricot interfacing such as Fusi Knit. Cut a length of interfacing long enough to extend 1 in. past both ends of the pocket opening, then position it along the edge of the pocket opening on the wrong side of the fabric and fuse it in place.*
2. *Staystitch on the seamline through the circles marking the ends of the pocket opening, then clip the seam allowance to each circle (see the illustration on the facing page).*
3. *Press the raw edge to the wrong side between the clips.*
4. *Next, topstitch the pocket opening by starting at the fold, pivoting, and sewing using a ¼-in. seam allowance, pivoting again, and ending at the fold. Lock in the stitch at each end by sewing in place using a zero stitch length.*
5. *Matching circles, pin the right side of the pocket to the wrong side of the front.*
6. *To mark the pocket stitching line, machine-baste or pin-baste from the wrong side, following the edge of the pocket as a guide. If you are pin-basting, use a fabric marker to mark the pin line on the right side of the garment, repin from the right side, and remove the back pins.*
7. *Topstitch using the basting or the marked line as a guide (see the illustration on the facing page). Be sure to topstitch next to the basting so the basting stitches can be easily removed. Continue sewing the garment as usual.*

Single-Layer Window Pockets

Window pockets are very versatile because they can be placed anywhere on a garment. The pocket opening may have a basic slotted shape, a modern geometric shape, or a curvy or free-form organic shape. I often use a simple slotted shape on pull-on pants that do not have side seams, sometimes with a vertical opening and sometimes with a diagonal opening, but on jackets and tops it's fun to use more decorative shapes. Decide on the pocket placement by pin-fitting the pattern and marking the best position. Otherwise use the existing pocket placement and just change the shape of the pocket opening.

You can use a self-facing or a fusible tricot interfacing as the facing to finish the pocket opening and self-fabric or a contrasting fabric as the actual pocket pouch. The pocket pouch is stitched through to the outside of the garment and stays neat and flat.

1. *To sew a single-layer window pocket, mark the shape of the pocket opening, which is also the stitching line for the pocket facing, on the garment pattern. A hip pocket should be a functional size that fits the wearer's hand. Pockets higher up on the bodice or just below the shoulders may be smaller than the hand.*
2. *To make a facing pattern for the pocket opening, pin plain pattern tissue on top of the garment pattern, and trace the pocket opening stitching line and grainline onto the*

pattern tissue. Unpin the pattern tissue and draw the outer facing edges 1 in. to 1½ in. wider than the pocket width and length.

3. Make a pattern for the pocket pouch by copying the shape of the pocket opening and the grainline onto a layer of pattern tissue.

The actual pocket pouch is a separate fabric layer placed behind the pocket opening that is large enough to fit the hand. The pocket pouch's shape may be square, rectangular, oval, or it may echo the shape of the pocket opening.

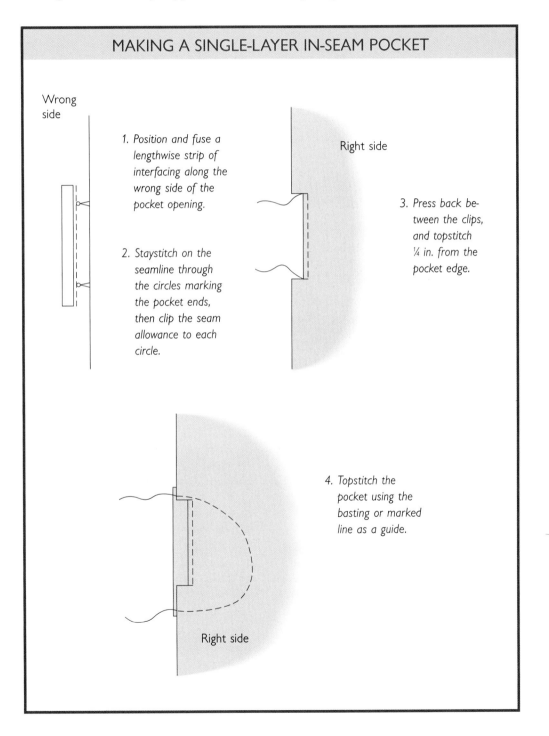

MAKING A SINGLE-LAYER IN-SEAM POCKET

Wrong side

1. Position and fuse a lengthwise strip of interfacing along the wrong side of the pocket opening.

2. Staystitch on the seamline through the circles marking the pocket ends, then clip the seam allowance to each circle.

Right side

3. Press back between the clips, and topstitch ¼ in. from the pocket edge.

4. Topstitch the pocket using the basting or marked line as a guide.

Right side

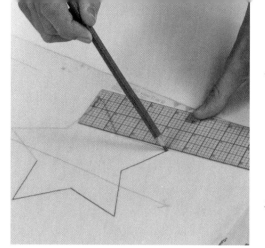

To make a facing pattern for a single-layer pocket opening, place blank pattern tissue on top of the garment pattern, and copy the pocket opening and the grainline onto the facing pattern.

4. Next, cut the pocket facing out of fashion fabric and out of a lightweight and fusible nonwoven interfacing. Alternately, you can fuse the interfacing to the wrong side of the facing fabric, then cut the pocket facing and interfacing in one step. It is especially useful to cut this way when the shape of the pocket opening is decorative and irregular.

5. If you cut the facing and interfacing separately, transfer the pocket opening stitching line to the smooth (nonadhesive) side of the fusible interfacing, and fuse the interfacing to the wrong side of the facing. If the fashion fabric is thick, bypass the self-fabric and use just the fusible interfacing as the facing. In this case, mark the pocket opening's stitching line on the wrong (adhesive) side of the fusible interfacing.

6. Pin the pocket facing on the right side of the garment. If you are using fusible interfacing only as the facing, pin its smooth side to the right side of the garment. Stitch along the marked stitching line.

7. Slash through the middle of the pocket through all layers, and clip any inside curves and to any corners. If the pocket has a contour shape, trim away the fabric from the center of the pocket opening, leaving a ¼-in. seam allowance.

8. If you are using a fabric facing, press it flat, then turn the pocket to the wrong side and press the pocket edge, being sure to roll

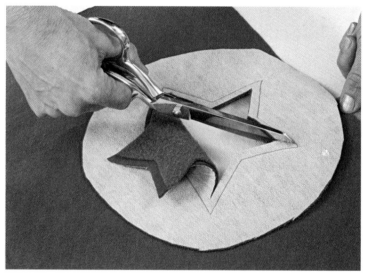

Because this pocket has a contour shape, trim the fabric away from the center of the pocket opening, leaving a ¼-in. seam allowance. The seam allowances should be clipped to all corners and curves.

Topstitch around the pocket opening using a single, double, or triple needle.

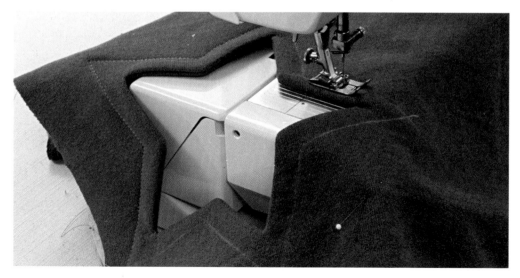

After attaching the pocket pouch, stitch down the inactive edge of the pocket opening (typically the top edge or the side edge that is away from the wide part of the pocket pouch). Sew on top of the previous topstitching, being sure to lock in the stitches.

the seamline slightly to the back. If you are using interfacing, turn the interfacing to the inside of the pocket, and carefully press the edge of the pocket opening in an up-and-down motion to tack the interfacing neatly to the back side of the pocket opening. Using a press cloth, fuse it in place permanently.

9. Finally, topstitch around the pocket opening using a single, double, or triple needle.

The pocket pouch sewing line may be completely different from the topstitching line around the window pocket, or the window pocket and the pocket pouch may have a topstitching line in common. What looks best depends on the combination of shapes that you are using as well as the placement on the garment. I find that having one common side is useful if the pocket opening has an unusual shape because the pocket stitching line does not compete with the pocket opening stitching line but instead becomes a continuation of it.

To attach the pocket pouch, position the right side of the pouch on the wrong side of the pocket opening, baste or pin-baste near the outer edge, then topstitch from the right side. It is useful to stitch down the upper, inactive edge of the pocket to the pocket pouch to keep it neat. Do this either by sewing a second row of stitching on top of the first topstitching or by topstitching the pocket window in two stages.

First topstitch the side of the pocket window that must remain open in order to insert your hand (typically the side closest to the bottom or center of the garment). Sew the remaining side through all layers after positioning the pocket pouch under the pocket opening.

PIECING FABRIC AND COLOR BLOCKING

There are endless ways to piece fabric. You can have a structured or a relaxed approach to color blocking, depending on how much you want to control the results. Sometimes control is necessary, but a bit of surprise may create interesting results. If you are a quilter, you have a head start in piecing and can try some of your techniques on wool jersey or piece together an assortment of knits having different colors and textures but compatible weights. Here are three approaches to piecing garments.

With the first method, you can easily create a color-blocked garment by dividing the pattern into sections. The second method is a little more freewheeling: You sew a pleasing color-blocked section of fabric first, then strategically place the pattern on the fabric following the straight of grain or the true bias. The last method, which uses spliced seams, allows you to color-block using curves, sharp points, and totally free-form or organic shapes. Spliced seams are overlapped appliqué seams that make it easy to sew more complex shapes.

> **TIP**
>
> If you like clothing with lots of color, pieced fabrics, and color-blocked clothing, then jersey, especially wool jersey, is a wonderful medium to use because it's almost as stable as a woven fabric while having the malleability of a knit. Wool jersey makes it possible to create nicely contoured clothes without having to do a lot of fitting, which means your pieced clothing doesn't have to have a boxy silhouette.

Basic Color Blocking

This is the structured approach to color blocking. Basic color blocking is a very systematic way to piece a garment. You start with the pattern, divide it into sections, add seam allowances, and cut the pieces using the original grainline.

1. *To color-block a front, back, or sleeve, make a full copy of the master pattern, and mark the piecing seamlines on the new paper pattern.*
2. *Pin-fit the pattern tissue to help you decide if the seams are in a flattering place on the body. I first use disappearing fabric marker to mark the lines on the pattern, then I switch to a pencil or permanent marker after deciding which is the best placement.*
3. *After drawing the seamlines, draw in the grainline on each section. The grainline should be an extension of the grainline that is already there or a line parallel to the original grainline.*

4. *Label each new section, and cut the pattern apart along the new seamlines.*
5. *Next, add a ¼-in. seam allowance to the newly cut edges (see the illustration on p. 86). It is best to add pattern tissue and actually mark in the new cutting line to include the seam allowance, but if you decide to add the seam allowance as you cut, be sure to mark "Add seam allowance" prominently on the pattern or you may forget to do it. To sew the ¼-in. seams, use either double-stitched seams, a stretch-overlock stitch, or a serger.*

Creating a Fabric

This is the relaxed approach. In this less-structured way to color-block, you sew blocks of fabric together that are just large enough to fit each pattern section, then cut with the center of the garment on the straight of grain or the true bias. I work with squares, rectangles, and triangles of different sizes. The sizes of the pieces don't matter, but each seam should be either on the lengthwise grain, the crossgrain, or the true bias. You can even make use of your leftover pieces of fabric if you have straightened the grain. If you work with small, quilt-patch-size fabric pieces, don't worry about the grain.

1. *Start by copying the master pattern onto pattern tissue so that you can work with a full front and a full back pattern.*
2. *Play with the fabric by arranging different colors and shapes on a table. To get an idea of how a garment piece will look with each arrangement, place the transparent paper pattern on top of the fabric, trying the lengthwise, crosswise, and all four bias directions to see which looks best (see the illustration on p. 87).*
3. *Once you've decided on an arrangement you like, stitch the pieces together using a ¼-in. seam allowance and double-stitched seams, a stretch-overlock stitch, or a serger.*
4. *After the fabric pieces are stitched together, place the paper pattern on top, trying different directions until you decide which position is best. In all, there are eight possible*

Try piecing sev-
eral same-size
patches using
the same color
combinations
but different
configurations.

BASIC COLOR BLOCKING

*After drawing the seamlines, draw the grainline on each section. Label
each section, then cut the pattern apart along the new seamlines.*

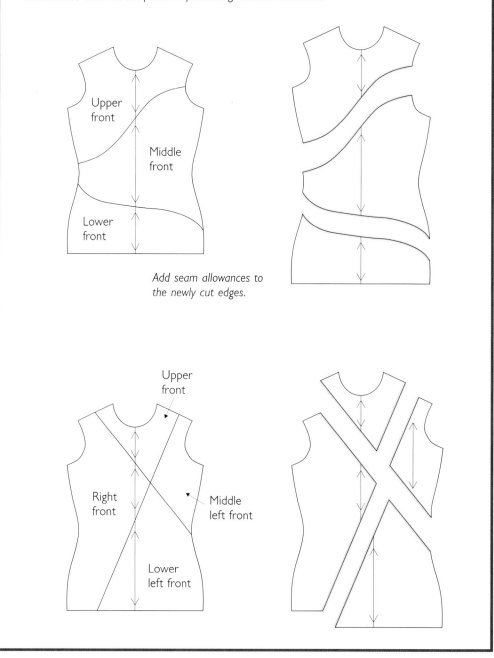

*Add seam allowances to
the newly cut edges.*

LAID-BACK COLOR BLOCKING

These are some ways you can arrange your garment pieces when using the relaxed approach to color blocking.

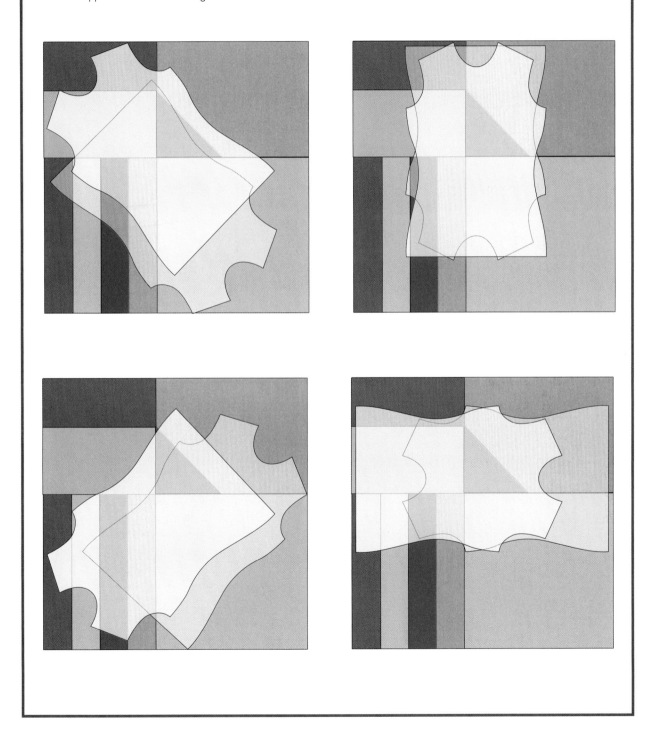

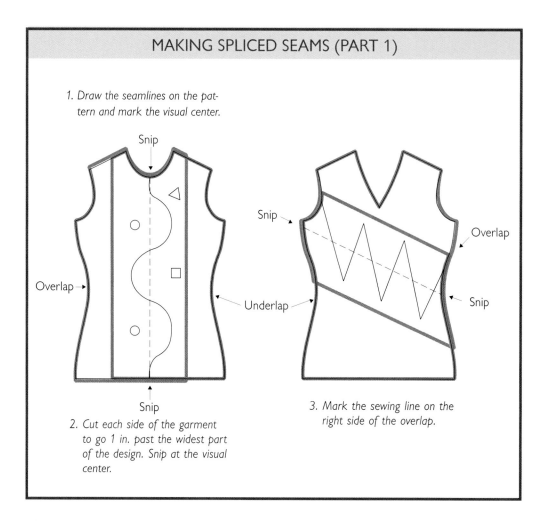

MAKING SPLICED SEAMS (PART 1)

1. Draw the seamlines on the pattern and mark the visual center.

Snip

Overlap →

← Overlap

Snip

Snip

Underlap

Overlap

Snip

Snip

2. Cut each side of the garment to go 1 in. past the widest part of the design. Snip at the visual center.

3. Mark the sewing line on the right side of the overlap.

TIP

When creating a color-blocked fabric, appliqué can be the final step to a good design by adding additional colors and shape after the fabric is pieced together. Appliquéd color can overlap other pieced areas without restrictions.

directions in which to place the pattern: two vertical, two horizontal, and four bias directions. If the pieced fabric is made a little larger than necessary, the pattern can also be moved left to right and up and down in each direction, allowing for even more placement variations.

Spliced Seams

An easy way to piece difficult contour seams is to use what I call spliced seams, which are appliquéd seams that are overlapped, stitched, and trimmed. Spliced seams allow you to do both positive and negative appliqué. You should work with a full front and a full back pattern, even if the design is balanced, so you can see the full design.

1. Begin by drawing your design seamlines on the paper pattern. To try out different ideas, use a disappearing fabric marker first or a separate paper overlay to avoid having undesired lines on the final pattern.
2. Once you've decided on the final design, permanently mark on the pattern, then find

4. To sew, position the wrong side overlap on top of the right side underlap, being sure to overlap the center matchpoints. Pin or baste the cut edges in place, then sew on the marked sewing lines.

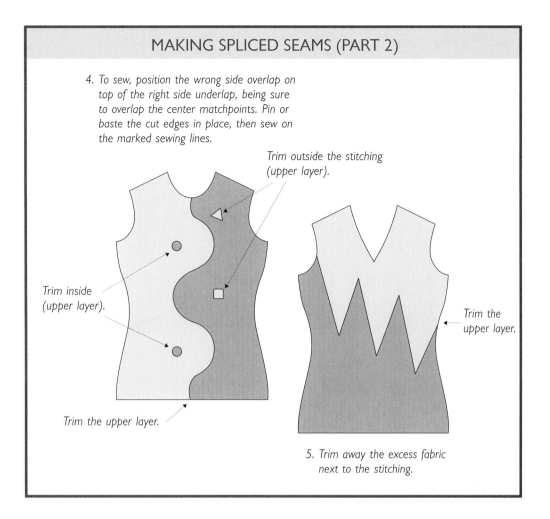

Trim outside the stitching (upper layer).

Trim inside (upper layer).

Trim the upper layer.

Trim the upper layer.

5. Trim away the excess fabric next to the stitching.

and mark the visual center of the design. It doesn't have to be the exact center, but it will be a matchpoint for overlapping and sewing the fabric pieces together.

3. Be sure to lay out and cut each section so that the right side of the pattern and the fabric face up. Cut each side of the garment to go 1 in. past the widest part of the design. To create matchpoints, snip the fabric where the visual center meets the edges of the fabric (see the illustration on the facing page).

4. Using dressmaker carbon, mark the sewing line on the right side of the overlap side of the garment.

5. Position the wrong side of the overlap on top of the right side of the remaining side, overlapping the center matchpoints. Pin or baste the cut edges together.

6. Next, sew the design lines in place using a straight or a zigzag stitch, then selectively trim away the top layer of fabric next to the stitching line. For example, if an area is completely defined by the stitching line, such as the circles, the square, and the triangle are in the illustration above, you may cut away the top layer of fabric inside the stitching line to expose the underneath color. Or you could cut away the top layer of fabric surrounding the stitching line so that the top color floats on the underlap color.

7. On the wrong side of the garment, trim away excess fabric, staying ¼ in. away from the stitching line.

5

Sewing Sweaterknits, Ribs, and Openwork Raschel Knits

Ribbed knits, sweaterknits, and some raschel knits have the homespun look of hand-knitted fabrics. The stitch formations include the basic and familiar rib stitch, bulky single knits, jacquard patterns, as well as other fancier varieties that look like hand-knitting stitches and hand-crochet lace.

RIBBED KNITS

Before spandex and fabrics with two-way stretch were developed, ribbed knits were the best way to create close-fitting garments that hug the body yet let you move with comfort. Ribbed fabrics are versatile, have hidden stretch, look modern, and have textured columns of vertical ribs that are slimming on any figure.

Ribbed knits can be used for an entire garment to easily achieve a body-conscious shape. The silhouette can be skintight or it can just skim the body, depending on the width of the pattern being used. Because ribbing easily conforms to curves and helps garment edges hug the body, it is an excel-

lent choice to use as finishing trim or binding on necklines, edges, and cuffs of both knits and woven fabrics.

Ribbed knits have pronounced vertical ridges on both sides of the fabric that are formed by alternating purl and plain stitches. A 1x1 rib alternates one purl stitch with one plain stitch, a 2x2 rib alternates two purl stitches with two plain stitches, and a 4x4 rib alternates four of each stitch and creates a wider rib. The resulting fabric looks narrow on a bolt but has lots of crosswise stretch.

A ribbed-knit garment can be considerably smaller than the body it is meant to fit. A close-fitting, pull-on, ribbed top measuring 12 in. across will fit a 24-in. waist when relaxed and easily expand to fit a 36-in. or more bust or hip. There are variations in the stretch, depending on the size of the rib and the type of fiber. If you compare a 4x4 rib and a 1x1 rib knitted from the same fiber and with the same number of stitches across, the 4x4 rib looks narrower than the 1x1 rib but stretches to the same maximum width. Conversely, if

TIP

Ready-to-wear tops made from ribbed fabric typically have straight side seams that follow a lengthwise rib; the armscye is also straight, except for the underarm curve. By contrast, full-fashioned ribbed sweaters often have shaped side seams attained by increasing and decreasing the number of stitches.

you compare two same-size squares of 4x4 and 1x1 ribbing, the 4x4 ribbing has more built-in stretch and more actual width when stretched.

Ribbings made of different fibers have different characteristics. Wool ribbing has excellent stretch and recovery. Cotton ribbing is firm but tends to loosen up or stretch out as you wear it, then gets tight again when you wash it. Polyester ribbing has a firm hand and retains its shape, while silk and rayon ribbing are soft and less resilient than the others. Adding spandex to all of these fibers increases the elasticity and shape retention.

Adapting a Pattern

The easiest ways to create a pattern for a ribbed top are to copy a store-bought top or to modify a leotard pattern or any close-fitting pattern meant for fabrics containing spandex. To copy a finished garment, use the same method discussed in "Copying a T-shirt or sweater" on pp. 22-24.

Adapting or modifying a leotard pattern for sewing ribbed fabrics is easy to do and will improve the sewing and fit of the ribbed top. If you were to select a typical commercial pattern meant for knits, you probably would not be pleased with the results because most patterns have shaped side seams and armscyes that curve too much for ribbed fabric.

What is so wonderful about using ribbing is that you can cut a perfectly rectangular top and it will conform to your shape. For a custom fit, you must first determine the width you need by checking the amount of stretch in the ribbing. For the body of the garment, take your bust, waist, and hip measurements and divide them in half. Let's say the bust is 36 in., the waist is 26 in., and the hips are 38 in. Divide these measurements in half to get 18 in., 13 in., and 19 in.

Next, fold the ribbing fabric crosswise about 6 in. from the cut edge, and see if half the waist measurement (13 in.) will

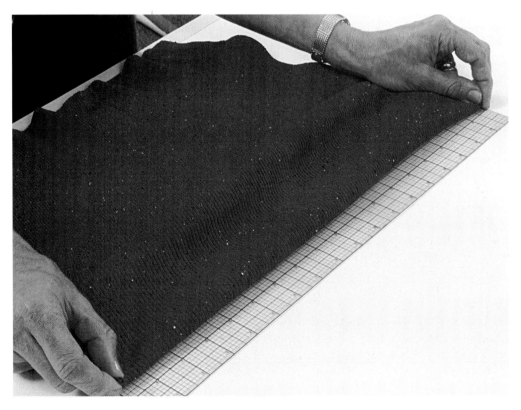

Check to see if ribbed fabric measuring half your waist measurement will stretch enough to fit half your bust and hip measurements. If the fabric stretches well beyond those measurements, you may wish to work with a narrower pattern. If it doesn't stretch enough, you will need to increase the width of the pattern.

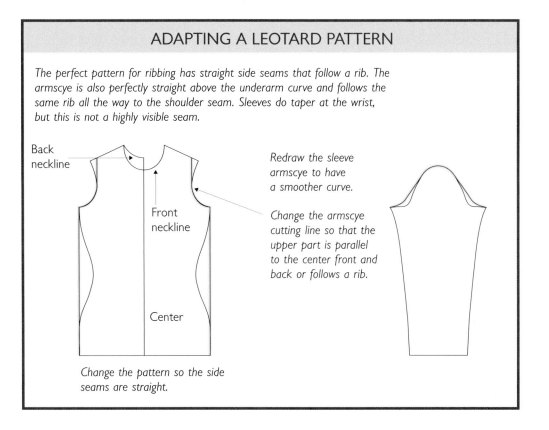

ADAPTING A LEOTARD PATTERN

The perfect pattern for ribbing has straight side seams that follow a rib. The armscye is also perfectly straight above the underarm curve and follows the same rib all the way to the shoulder seam. Sleeves do taper at the wrist, but this is not a highly visible seam.

Back neckline

Front neckline

Center

Change the pattern so the side seams are straight.

Redraw the sleeve armscye to have a smoother curve.

Change the armscye cutting line so that the upper part is parallel to the center front and back or follows a rib.

stretch to fit the bust (18 in.) and hips (19 in.) without distorting. If the ribbing is very elastic, it may be that 11 in. or 12 in. of ribbing will also fit the bust and hip measurements.

Now you must decide how close-fitting you would like the garment to be. If you decide to have a less form-fitting but still shaped silhouette, you can make your pattern 1 in. to 3 in. wider than the waist measurement. Larger sizes may prefer a more relaxed fit. For a relaxed fit, cut the garment to be the same width or just a few inches less than the bust or hip measurement but always keep the side seams straight. This way the garment will hug the bust but gently skim over the rest of the body.

Once you establish the width you want to use, select the leotard pattern size that is closest to that width, and copy or change the pattern so that the side seams are

straight. Larger sizes can use a T-shirt pattern meant for knits with moderate stretch.

It is easiest to use the same pattern for both the front and the back, changing just the neckline. If the upper part of the armscye curves away from the center and widens at the shoulders, change the cutting line so that the upper part of the armscye is parallel to the center front and back and follows a rib (see the illustration above). Eliminate the center back seam if there is one. I like to allow ½-in. seam allowances that I trim with my serger (or after stitching the seams on a conventional machine) and 1-in. hem allowances.

Cutting Ribbing

The easiest and most accurate way to cut a top out of ribbing is to first cut a rectangle of fabric that is the width and length of the finished top plus seam and hem allowances. Because the ribs expand and contract, cut the second one the same width by counting the number of raised ribs across instead of measuring. Keep in mind that adding or subtracting just a few extra ribs can add or subtract many more hidden inches. Every rib counts.

TIP

You do not have to count ribs when cutting 1x1 rib fabric because it has a stable width. You can use a measurement instead, but it is still a good idea to cut two rectangles of fabric one at a time.

With two rectangles of ribbing lined up with right sides together, outline and cut the front and back using the higher neckline. Then use the pattern to cut separately one layer with the lower neckline.

Knitwear manufacturers mark the desired width by drawing a lengthwise needle, which is like dropping a stitch, when they knit the fabric, giving the cutter an established width mark to follow. This way the side seams follow a rib exactly.

Once you have cut two rectangles of fabric, you may line them up with right sides facing and cut both front and back armscyes together. The front and back neckline are typically different and must be cut individually. For the sleeves, cut two rectangles of fabric equal in width to the widest part of the sleeve pattern and long enough to fit the pattern length. Once again, count ribs to be sure the widths are equal. Line up the cloth rectangles with right sides facing and cut the sleeves.

Sewing Ribbing

You can sew ribbed garments on a sewing machine using narrow double-stitched seams, an overlock stitch, or a stretch-overlock stitch. If the ribbing is a fine gauge and closely knitted, ¼-in. seam allowances are fine. For other ribbed knits, a ½-in. or ⅝-in. seam allowance allows you to sew neater seams because you trim the excess seam allowance after sewing the seam on a sewing machine. You can also use a three- or four-thread serger stitch to sew and trim the seam simultaneously. Crosswise seams, such as those at the shoulder, are easy to stretch out of shape, so help them retain their shape as well as their stretch by stabilizing with them with clear elastic (see pp. 70-73).

Hemming ribbed garments presents a dilemma. The hemming stitch needs to be able to stretch like the ribbing without looking stretched out, although if you are sewing a close-fitting garment, it may not matter if the hem looks a little stretched off the body. What is most important is how the hem looks when you are wearing the garment.

It is easy to find matching or coordinating ribbing in basic cotton, but fashion fabrics and fashion colors may prove to be more of a challenge to match. You could use an alternative edge finish, but sometimes ribbing is selected for its look as well as for its function. If the fashion fabric you are using has good stretch and, better yet, good recovery, you can sew a matching faux ribbing from it. Faux ribbing is made by sewing parallel rows of stitches using a double needle to imitate the look and function of real ribbing. It may not stretch as much as the real thing, but you can use it as a substitute when self-fabric trim is indicated on the pattern.

Double needles come in a variety of sizes and different widths. To make faux ribbing, use the widest width possible that is compatible with the throat plate of your machine, typically 4mm or 6mm. The greater the space between the needles, the more prominent the ridges you create will be. Use 100% polyester thread for strength and elasticity.

First, make test samples to experiment with different spacing between the rows of stitching, stitch length, and tension. Mark the settings on the test sample so that you can compare them later on and have a reference. If the ridge that is formed between the needles is not prominent enough, try shortening the stitch length and tightening the tension. To increase the

Faux ribbing always matches perfectly because it is sewn using the fashion fabric.

It is efficient to sew each row in an alternating direction. Do this by turning the fabric around at the end of the row and pulling the thread just enough to start sewing the next without having to cut the thread.

elasticity, try woolly nylon or elastic thread in the bobbin.

I try to create the minimum amount of ribbing necessary for a project plus a little extra for testing stitches and buttonholes. Determine the length of ribbing you need, and piece strips together as you go. The width of the ribbing should equal two times the desired width plus two generous seam allowances. I use ⅝-in. or ¾-in. seam

(continued on p. 96)

STRATEGICALLY PLACED RIBBING

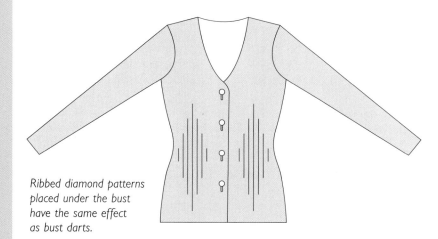

Ribbed diamond patterns placed under the bust have the same effect as bust darts.

Where the strategically placed ribbing ends in the middle of the garment instead of at the fabric edge, you can lock in the stitch by sewing in place using a zero stitch length. Then pull the top threads to the back, tie them together, and cut away the excess thread.

allowances so the edges can be recut if they look wavy.

One of the advantages of creating your own trim is that you can eliminate the ribbing from some seam allowances. If using ribbing on a cardigan, for example, stop the ribbing at the hemline so the seam allowances at the lower edge will be flat.

Start sewing the first row of ribbing at the center of the ribbing band or at one of the seams if you've pieced some strips together. I find it efficient to sew each row in an alternating direction, starting each row

¼ in. in from the edge to get a good grip on the fabric, then ending at the cut edge. Turn the fabric around, and sew a parallel row in the opposite direction, pulling the thread just enough to start sewing the next row without having to cut the thread.

If the bottom elastic or thread runs out in the middle of a row, pull the top threads to the back of the fabric by pulling the back thread until the top threads loop through to the back. Pull each loop with the tip of a pin to pull the threads to the back, then tie the top and

back threads together. Start sewing again with a full bobbin, overlapping the last stitching by a few stitches. When you finish sewing, pull these threads to the back and tie with the bobbin thread.

You can also use faux ribbing in strategically placed areas of a garment. Since ribbing pulls in the shape of a garment, the waist and midriff areas are ideal locations for it. The illustrations above and on the facing page will give you some placement ideas.

If you are using a serger, use a blind-hemming stitch or flatlock the hem. The false blind hem on a serger tends to emphasize the crosswise stretch and is not appropriate. If you are using a sewing machine, use a zigzag stitch and a blind-hem presser foot to blind hem, starting with a setting that is

2mm wide and long but reducing the width as much as possible to create the least visible stitch. To increase the elasticity of the stitch when you topstitch the hem, use woolly nylon or elastic thread in the bobbin.

Another hem option that is used in ready-to-wear is a machine or serger lettuce

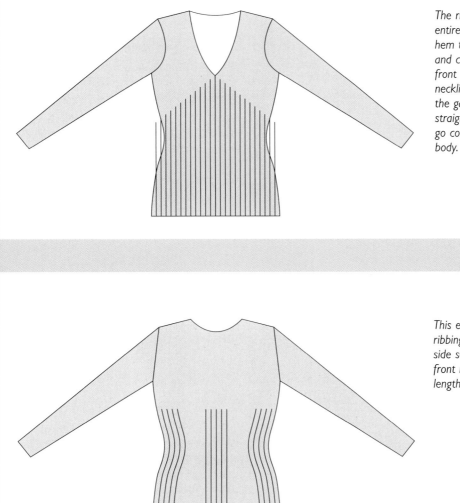

The ribbing goes around the entire garment from the hem to just below the bust and curves up at the center front to form a point at the neckline. The side seams of the garment must be straight to have the ribbing go completely around the body.

This example shows the side ribbing parallel to the curved side seams and the center front ribbing following the lengthwise grain.

hem. Because ribbing has lots of stretch, this method gives an attractive fluted effect at the hem.

Necklines and edges may be finished using ribbing, binding, elastic, or just by turning and stitching. Once again, woolly nylon thread is an asset in keeping the seams as elastic as possible. Shaped facings are not an option on ribbed garments unless you are willing to completely eliminate the stretch from the garment neckline. This would only be possible if the ribbed garment is not close fitting.

SWEATERKNITS AND SWEATERBODIES

Why knit sweaters from scratch when you can sew beautiful ones that suit your style just by using a conventional sewing machine or a serger? If there is one knitted fabric that even veteran sewers are likely to shy away from using it is the sweaterknit. The reasons may be due to two

misconceptions: first, that it is not possible to machine-sew sweaters, and second, that you must have matching trim. These notions are far from reality. Sweaters are easy to sew once you establish the best stitch settings, and it's easy to use self-fabric or purchased trim to finish necklines and edges.

When sewing bulky knits, the best styles avoid making the body look bulky. Choose short, cropped styles that end from just above to just below the waist, or select large, long styles that are obviously over-sized. Bulky fabrics are best for outerwear such as unstructured jackets, cardigans, top-pers, and coats, while oversized styles layer nicely over other clothing. Cashmere and lamb's wool sweaterknits are not bulky and make warm and beautiful one- and two-piece dresses, skirts, unstructured suits, and twinset sweater combinations. Openwork raschel laces can be used for one- and two-piece dresses, tops, tunics, and open-front cardigan styles that rival hand-crocheted garments.

Choosing a Pattern

Although it is unusual to find patterns specifically for sweaterknits, you can adapt any pattern meant for stretch or woven fabrics by considering the amount of stretch in the sweaterknit when you choose the size, and by changing the way you finish seams, necklines, and edges. Keeping the pattern simple is the key to getting great results. Copying your favorite sweater is a second option (see pp. 22-24).

Knitting books are a good source for style and pattern ideas since they typically offer a photograph or a drawing of the fin-ished sweater just like a sewing pattern. The schematics for the finished shapes or pattern are easy to follow, even for non-knitters. You can use them to make an actual paper pattern, or you can draw the sweater shape directly onto the sweater-knit, but you must add seam and hem allowances because hand-knitted garments don't have them.

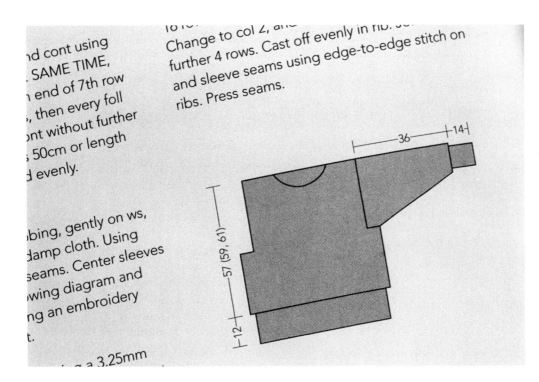

Partial text within the diagram:

...d cont using
...SAME TIME,
...end of 7th row
..., then every foll
...nt without further
...; 50cm or length
...d evenly.

...bing, gently on ws,
...damp cloth. Using
...seams. Center sleeves
...wing diagram and
...ng an embroidery
...t.

...a 3.25mm

Change to col 2, a...
further 4 rows. Cast off evenly in rib. J...
and sleeve seams using edge-to-edge stitch on
ribs. Press seams.

36 | 14
57 (59, 61) | 12

Knitting books are a great source of patterns for sweaterknits and sweaterbodies. The schematics show the pattern shapes with measurements, but you must add seam and hem allowances because hand-knitted garments don't have them.

Cutting Sweaterknits

When cutting sweaterknits, mark any notches or matchpoints using tailor's chalk or an air-erasable marker. T-pins are especially useful on bulky and loosely knitted fabrics because they are less likely to sink in and get lost in the fabric, which might cause machine problems when you sew.

Most sweaterknits have large yarns, and the stitches unravel easily compared with other knits. You should cut sweaterknits with normal seam allowances of ½ in. or ⅝ in., or cut them wider if you buy a fabric that is very loosely knitted. If the pattern you are using has ¼-in. seam allowances, increase the allowances, then trim away the excess after sewing the seams. A serger will automatically trim the seams as you sew.

Sewing Sweaterknits

When sewing seams on a sewing machine, you can manage the thickness of the fabric by pushing the fabric toward the foot to help it feed, by reducing the pressure of the presser foot, or, better still, by using a walking foot. Use double-stitched seams when sewing on a sewing machine. A narrow or medium zigzag ranging from 0.5mm to 2mm wide and 2.5mm long works well for the first stitching. For the second stitching, use a medium or wide zigzag ranging from 2mm to 5mm wide and 3mm long, then trim away the excess seam allowance next to this stitching.

Alternatively, you could use a double-overlock or stretch-overlock stitch placed on the seamline, then trim away the excess seam after sewing. Do a test seam to be sure the settings produce an elastic seam, but don't stretch it out of shape. Lengthen the stitch if the seam looks wavy or stretched.

The three- or four-thread serger stitches both work well on sweaterknits, but it is important to adjust the differential feed to avoid stretching the seam as you sew. To start each seam on a serger, feed the sweaterknit with the foot and the knife up because of the thickness of the fabric, then lower the foot and begin sewing. Use the left needle when using the three-thread serger stitch to sew bulky knits. For stability, I like to use a narrow sewing-machine zigzag stitch combined with a three-thread

TIP

A walking foot is an invaluable sewing aid when sewing bulky fabrics.

Copying a sweater is just as easy as copying a T-shirt. Since sweaterbodies typically have ribbing at the bottom that pulls the sweater in, I find it easier to make a partial pattern for the body, stopping the pattern a few inches below the armscye. Follow the directions on pp. 22-24 for copying a T-shirt, but stop the pattern 4 in. to 6 in. below the armscye. Make a note of the finished length on the pattern.

To cut the sweater, cut two blocks of fabric following the lengthwise ribs of the sweaterknit and equal to the widest part of the sweater pattern. Cut the front and back individually, or stack up the two pieces with right sides facing and place the pattern on top, positioning the upper edge far enough from the bottom to give you the length you want the finished sweater to be (see the illustration below). Cutting the sweaterbody this way gives you the perfectly straight side seams that are typical in sweaters.

Although ribbing is normally used on the bottom of a sweater, on sleeves, and to finish the neckline, you have other more interesting options. If a knitted fabric is stable, you can use it sideways so that the ribbing follows the front edge of a cardigan or diagonally when sewing a wrap-front sweater. Placing the ribbing in the shoulder area creates a yoke effect. Any ribbing that gets cut away can be used as trim. If the bottom edge isn't finished with ribbing, it must be hemmed with a blind-hemming stitch or a catchstitch.

USING A PARTIAL PATTERN TO COPY A SWEATER

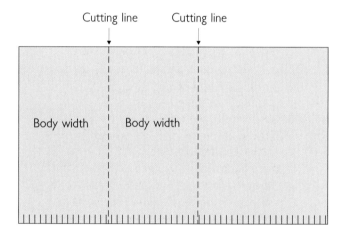

Following the lengthwise ribs of a sweaterbody, cut two blocks of fabric equal to the widest part of the sweater pattern.

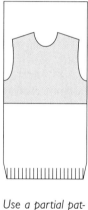

Use a partial pattern that stops 4 in. to 6 in. below the armscye to cut the shape of the sweaterbody.

serger stitch rather than just using the serger stitch. Shoulder seams should be stabilized with bias tricot or clear elastic.

You can sew hems invisibly using a serger blind-hemming stitch or a machine blind-hemming stitch with a blind-hem foot and a zigzag stitch setting of 2mm wide and 2mm to 5mm long. To hem invisibly by hand, use a blind catchstitch. Topstitch hems on a machine by using single- or multiple-needle topstitching or on a serger by flatlocking.

Necklines and edges can be finished by turning back and topstitching or by applying binding, ribbing, or purchased trim. If the knitted fabric has enough stretch, self-fabric can be used as ribbing. When sewing stable sweaterknits, shaped facings can be used to finish necklines and edges as I did on the short tweed cardigan shown on p. 24, but you need to take the thickness of the sweaterknit into consideration.

Finishing the Front Edges

There are two easy techniques for finishing the front edges of a sweater that give the same look on the outside of the garment. The difference is in the thickness of the resulting front edge. If the sweaterknit is not too bulky, use a narrow self-facing. Fold the sweaterknit lengthwise to decide if the front will be too bulky. Remember that with a self-facing, the front edges of the cardigan will overlap when you close it, and there will be four layers of fabric there. If this would be too bulky, the second option is to use grosgrain ribbon to face the front edges, which creates a stable edge without adding any bulk.

Self-facing   To finish the front edge using a self-facing, be sure to allow an extra 1½ in. of width at the front edge when cutting the garment. This will be folded back to use as a narrow facing.

1. *Start by fusing 1½-in.-wide strips of fusible tricot interfacing cut on the crossgrain to the front facings up to the foldline (see the*

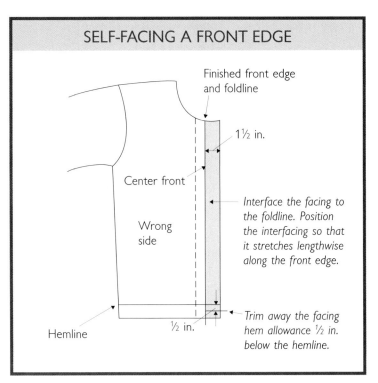

SELF-FACING A FRONT EDGE

Finished front edge and foldline

1½ in.

Center front

Wrong side

Interface the facing to the foldline. Position the interfacing so that it stretches lengthwise along the front edge.

Hemline

½ in.

Trim away the facing hem allowance ½ in. below the hemline.

illustration above). This allows some lengthwise stretch on the front edge.

2. *Finish the facing edge using a three-thread serger stitch, or trim the interfaced facing edge to neaten, then use a machine overlock stitch with an overedge foot.*

3. *If you are using a sweaterknit, hem the garment using a serger or a machine blind-hemming stitch, using plain or decorative topstitching, or by hand using a blind catchstitch. For best results, be sure the garment hem is no less than 1 in. and no more than 1½ in. wide. Trim the hem allowance on the front facing to ½ in., stopping at the front foldline. If you are using a sweaterbody, the hem is already finished.*

4. *Fold back the front facing, and edgestitch or slipstitch the lower fold.*

5. *Finish the neckline using binding or ribbing or by turning back and topstitching.*

Grosgrain facing   To keep the front edges stable and as flat as possible, use grosgrain ribbon as a facing. Grosgrain ribbon is readily available in a variety of colors and is stable enough for machine-sewn buttonholes without needing interfacing or other stabilizers. Attach the ribbon at the end of construction, after sewing the sweater together and finishing the neckline and hem.

1. *Using 1-in. to 1½-in.-wide ribbon, depending on the width of the overlap and the size of the buttons, cut two lengths of ribbon 2 in. longer than the garment's front edge.*
2. *On the right side of the garment, position the ribbon over the front opening. The ribbon should be 1 in. longer than the front edge at the top and bottom. If it isn't, you may have stretched the front edge, and you'll need to repin, easing in the front edge.*
3. *Topstitch the ribbon as close as possible to the edge (see the illustration below).*
4. *Fold the ribbon to the inside of the sweater so that it doesn't show on the right side, then fold back and stitch the raw edges of the ribbon, stitching in place to the ribbon layer only. You need to slipstitch the ribbon to the sweater only at the top and bottom of*

the front opening because the buttons and buttonholes will keep the ribbon in place.

Creating the Perfect Trim

You can use the unraveled yarns from sweaterknits to create a variety of trims that complement the fabric and the style you are sewing. The same material can give very different results. You can machine-couch the yarns to a binding fabric to make a corded trim, knit or crochet a matching trim, or bind off the edge of the sweaterknit using the same unraveled yarn.

Hand-knitting or crocheting trim for by-the-yard sweaterknits is a shortcut that gives the look of a hand-knit sweater. I won't be teaching you how to knit or crochet here, but these are possibilities if you already know how. I had never crocheted but was able to follow directions in a book for crocheting a picot edge.

In order to use the yarn, you will need to unravel the sweaterknit, which is easy to do once the crossgrain is straightened.

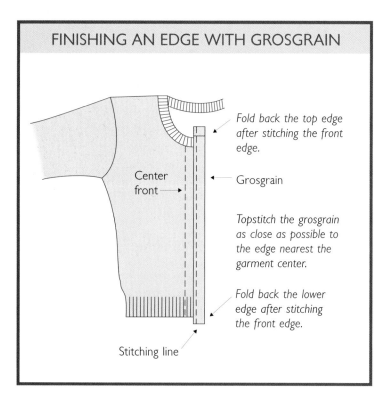

FINISHING AN EDGE WITH GROSGRAIN

Center front

Fold back the top edge after stitching the front edge.

Grosgrain

Topstitch the grosgrain as close as possible to the edge nearest the garment center.

Fold back the lower edge after stitching the front edge.

Stitching line

Some interesting options for finishing edges on sweaterknits include (from left to right) purchasing a complementary knitted trim, using unraveled yarns to knit or crochet a trim, and machine-couching the yarn to a binding fabric to create a bold corded edge.

When you can unloop a continuous row of stitches, you will know you have a straight edge and can start to wind the yarn.

Unraveling the fabric To unravel fabric, first determine in which direction the knit will unravel by pulling across the grain on the cut edge and trying to cause a stitch to run down or unloop. If it does unravel, start straightening and unraveling from this edge. If it does not unravel, go to the opposite cut edge.

Straighten the crossgrain by cutting as straight as possible along a course of knitted loops. When you can unloop a continuous row of stitches, you will know you have a straight edge and can start to wind the yarn. Wind the yarn around a piece of cardboard or around itself to form a ball.

When you unravel circular knits that have been cut apart, you will have to tie each row of yarn to the next row or yarn in order to have a continuous yarn. Flat knits unravel as a continuous length of yarn, going back and forth from one finished edge to the other.

To experiment, unravel 2 in. of fabric. You don't need to unravel very much fabric if you plan to use the yarns for couching, to crochet a narrow edge, or to bind off the hem. Ribbing requires the most yarn.

First, decide how wide your ribbing will be. Unraveling 2 in. of fabric is enough to knit a 2-in.-wide ribbing long enough to fit a garment or edge that is as long as the fabric's width. If your garment or edge is narrower than the fabric's width, you will have some extra yarn. If your garment or edge is twice as wide as the width of the fabric, you will need to unravel twice as much yarn. In either case, you will want to unravel 1 in. or 2 in. extra to practice with.

Making corded trim If the style you are sewing needs a defined edge trim, create a matching corded trim using unraveled strands from the knitted fabric. This cording is special because you select the yarns that match or best highlight the style you are sewing.

The base fabric must have some stretch so that the binding can follow the curves of

TIP

Fabrics are often knitted using one or more strands of yarn to form each stitch. To keep your trim the same thickness as the knitted fabric, wind and knit multiple strands together, treating them as a single yarn.

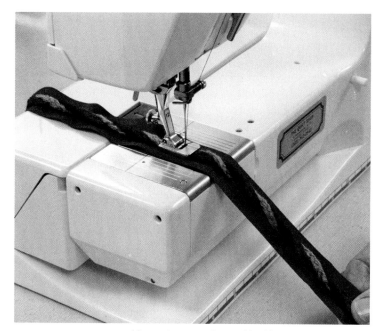

Use a zigzag stitch or a blind-hemming stitch to sew the cord to the center of the bias trim.

TIP

Before making a trim, practice, practice, practice to make sure you like the results. Start with a medium zigzag, then increase or decrease the width and length to suit your trim. The aim is to use as narrow a stitch as possible to couch the cording. The sample shown at left uses a 1mm stitch width and a 5mm stitch length with the needle positioned to the right of center. Doing this places the zigzag stitch on the right edge of the cording when you sew it to the trim fabric.

TIP

Mixing a purchased cord with unraveled yarns can help you increase the diameter of the new corded trim. Introducing a metallic, rayon, textured, or another color yarn will add some surface interest.

the neckline. Use a crosswise strip of self-fabric when possible. If the fashion fabric is very thick or has very little stretch, a bias woven fabric or purchased knitted trim can be used. Other alternatives include crosswise strips of coordinating lightweight jersey or 1¼-in.-wide purchased bias tricot trim. Narrow ½-in. to ¾-in. trims that stretch and have finished edges on one or both sides can also be used here. The base fabric does not have to be a perfect match because it will be on the inside of the neckline when you wear the garment.

1. Begin by twisting or braiding several strands of yarn to create a cord.
2. If using yardage, cut 1¼-in.-wide crosswise strips of stretch fabric or bias-cut woven fabric to use as the base fabric.
3. Couch strands of yarn to the center of the base fabric using a cording foot or a bead and sequin foot to guide the cord as you sew it in place (see the photo above). To sew, use a zigzag stitch or a blind-hemming stitch. If you are using a narrow trim with finished edges on one or both sides, couch the cord along the finished edge.

4. Fold the 1¼-in. trim in half lengthwise with the cording along the folded edge, then serge, zigzag, or machine-overlock the binding edges together (see the top photo on the facing page).
5. On the sweater neckline or edge you are finishing, allow a ⅝-in. seam allowance. Pin the trim to the right side of the seam, lining up the raw edges, then sew in place next to the cording using a zipper or cording foot (see the bottom photo on the facing page).
6. Turn the finished edges to the inside of the garment so the couched edge is along the neckline.
7. Finally, hold the trim in place by topstitching the neckline near the cording or by slipstitching the finished edges to the back side of the neckline.

Redesigning Old Sweaters

Once you are comfortable sewing sweaterknits, you can use these techniques to easily restyle sweaters and improve or update the style by changing the shape, the size, or the proportions of the garment. Common changes include improving the fit, reducing the width or length, changing the shoulder width and sleeve length, and converting a pullover into a cardigan by adding a zipper or button closure. These changes just rearrange the fabric that is already there.

Fold the trim lengthwise so the cording is along the folded edge, then serge, machine-overlock, or zigzag the edges together.

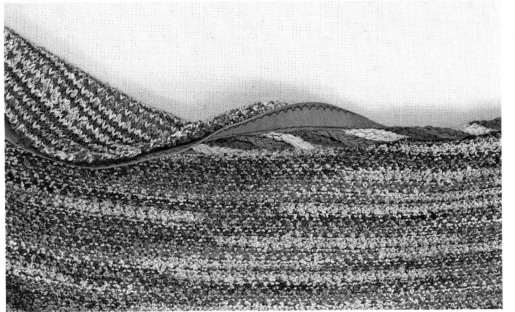

Pin the trim to the right side of the seam, lining up the raw edges, and sew in place next to the cording. Turn the edges to the inside of the garment so the cording falls along the garment edge.

BINDING OFF THE BOTTOM OF A KNIT

On medium to heavy knits, it is possible to bind off the stitches at the bottom of the garment. To do this, the hem must be straight and follow a course of stitches, so you must straighten the fabric before you cut the garment. First determine in which direction the knit will unravel by pulling across the grain on the cut edge, trying to cause a stitch to run or unloop. If it does unravel, start straightening and unraveling from this edge. If it does not unravel, go to the opposite cut edge.

Cut as straight as possible along the crossgrain, then unravel the knit until you have a complete row of loops. The garment should be cut so the lower edge of the pattern is ½ in. above the loops. Next, sew the

Use a crochet hook to close the loops by pulling the second stitch through the first stitch, then the third stitch through the second stitch, and so forth.

garment together as usual and finish the hems. Unravel the lower edge one or two more courses to expose a fresh row of loops, then use a crochet hook to close the loops by pulling the second stitch through the first and the third through the second, and so on. If you have never knitted before, this is just like finishing off a pot holder.

CHANGING A SWEATER'S WIDTH

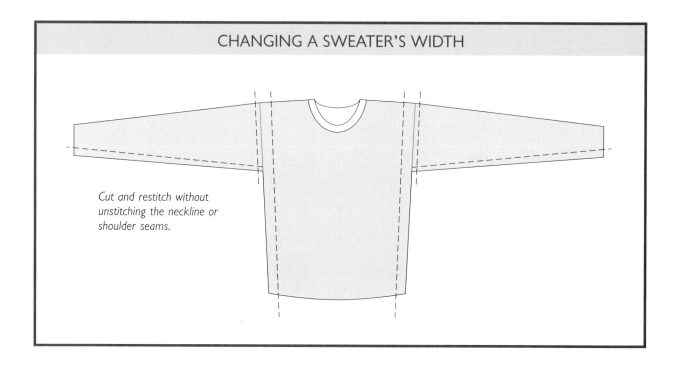

Cut and restitch without unstitching the neckline or shoulder seams.

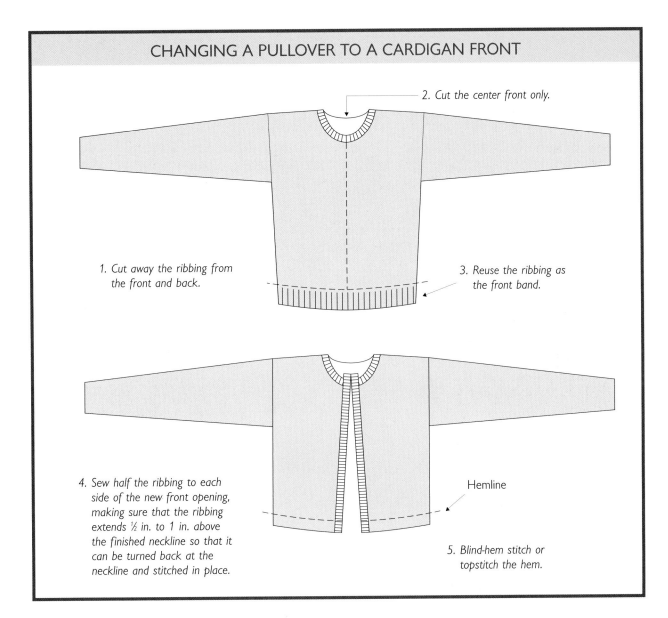

CHANGING A PULLOVER TO A CARDIGAN FRONT

2. Cut the center front only.

1. Cut away the ribbing from the front and back.

3. Reuse the ribbing as the front band.

4. Sew half the ribbing to each side of the new front opening, making sure that the ribbing extends ½ in. to 1 in. above the finished neckline so that it can be turned back at the neckline and stitched in place.

Hemline

5. Blind-hem stitch or topstitch the hem.

Creating a brand-new sweater by combining parts of used sweaters is fun to do and a terrific way to give new life to damaged, spotted, or partially worn garments. Save entire garments or just the parts with interesting trim, ribbing, unusual stitches, prints, and handwork to use again. For example, the floral appliqués on my gray-striped sweaterknit are recycled from an old Christian Dior sweater that I restyled (see the top photo on p. 108). Because I could not bring myself to throw away the printed fabric that was cut away on the restyled

sweater, I now have this delicate appliqué on the new cardigan that can be worn together with the restyled sweater.

Being able to restyle sweaters enables me to see store-bought sweaters and knitted or crocheted scarves as new sources for interesting fabrics and details that can easily transcend their current forms. Buying a brand-new cashmere sweater to restyle may not make the best sense, but many of those end-of-season sale sweaters are wonderful candidates for restyling.

KNITTED LACE AND OTHER OPENWORK KNITS

Most knitted laces and openwork knits are stable raschel knits that are very different from the stretch laces often used for T-shirts and lingerie. Knitted laces can be found in a variety of fibers, such as cotton, wool, acrylic, cotton/polyester, and rayon. Unlike laces with nylon or spandex, these have little crosswise stretch and no lengthwise stretch, although a little stretch is sometimes gained from the openness of the lace formations.

Knitted rayon laces have an elegant surface sheen and a drapey, slinky hand. Rayon laces need secure seams because the combination of openwork fabric construction, slippery rayon yarns, and narrow seams increases the tendency of the fabric to unravel easily. Cut these lace knits with a ½-in. or a ⅝-in. seam allowance, then cut away the excess seam after sewing.

Secure seams are easy to do if you modify the stitch settings you use to sew them. Use double-stitched seams, such as a narrow to medium zigzag stitch that is 1mm to 2.5mm wide and long combined with a three- or four-thread serger stitch. If seams are stretching or waving, increase the length of the sewing machine stitch and the differential feed of the serger. If you don't have a serger, try using a second zigzag, a double-overlock stitch, or a stretch overlock instead. Do a test seam to select the most appropriate combination for your lace.

Some openwork knits have very open areas or gaps along the seamline. In that case, use bias tricot such as Seams Great in a color that blends with the fashion fabric to connect the gaps so that you can sew and stabilize the seams. To do this, pin the seam with right sides together, then position the bias tricot so that it is centered over the seamline and it curls away from the fabric. Using a narrow or medium zigzag, sew the seam together with the tricot facing up, then finger-press the tricot toward the seam allowances. Sew or serge

To connect the gaps when sewing openwork knits, center some bias tricot trim over the seamline so that it curls away from the fashion fabric. With the tricot facing up, sew the seam together using a narrow to medium zigzag stitch.

After finger-pressing both edges of the tricot toward the garment seam allowances, sew or serge the second row of stitching next to the first, then cut away the excess seam allowance.

the second stitching next to the first, catching the tricot and cutting away the excess seam. Just a bit of tricot will remain in the actual seam.

Shoulder seams should be reinforced twice because they are more susceptible to strain than other seams. Using a stabilizer such as bias tricot or a strip of fusible tricot interfacing, sew the shoulder seam using a double-stitched seam combination, then topstitch the shoulder seam to one side using a zigzag stitch or a straight stitch.

To topstitch hems, use size 70 or 75 twin needles with a 2mm or 2.5mm space between the needles. You can also use a single-needle zigzag stitch that is either 2mm or 3mm wide and long.

Necklines can be finished by using clear elastic and one of the techniques on pp. 48-63 or by using binding or purchased trim. On my openwork lace sample, it was possible to apply self-binding at the neckline using a narrow binder attachment. Using a zigzag stitch instead of a straight stitch fastened the folded edges more securely to the neckline. If self-binding is not possible, consider using a lightweight bias woven fabric or crosswise-cut tricot or jersey to bind the edge, then turn the bound edge to the inside of the garment and topstitch the neckline.

When using a binder attachment to finish a neckline, use a zigzag stitch instead of a straight stitch to sew the binding in place. The zigzag stitch will securely fasten the openwork binding to the neckline.

6

Sewing Spandex and Other Specialty Knits

Special knits add variety, interest, and flair to your wardrobe. These knits go beyond the basic and familiar fabrics and stitches to include some fabrics and finishes that are not necessarily associated with knits. Knits such as swimsuit knits, stretch velvet, synthetic fleece, matte jersey, slinky knits, and other novelty knits require special attention in order to get the best results from them.

SWIMSUIT AND HIGH-SPANDEX KNITS

Can you imagine how different swimsuits and active sportswear would be without the use of spandex and two-way stretch fabrics? Because knitted fabrics with spandex have excellent stretch and, more important, excellent recovery, they allow you to create form-fitting garments that hold their shape without the need for zippers or other fasteners. High-spandex fabrics are not just for swimsuits and activewear. The increased use of spandex fiber in more and more knits results in more resilient fabrics that don't bag or sag when you wear them.

When using a high-spandex fabric, the pattern can and should be simple because

of the fabric's ability to mold around a person's shape. The best patterns for these fabrics take advantage of their good qualities. Since many spandex fabrics don't necessarily look like swimwear fabric, the garments you sew with them do not have to be swimwear. These fabrics are a great choice for sewing close-fitting garments that are comfortable to wear or for loose-fitting garments that hold their shape.

While spandex is added to a wide variety of wovens for comfort, this section is about knitted fabrics with lengthwise and crosswise stretch. Two-way and four-way stretch knits both have lots of lengthwise and crosswise stretch and are used interchangeably in garments. The difference lies in how each fabric is knitted. Four-way stretch knits tend to be thicker, more durable, and more elastic because the elasticity is derived from two sources: the structure of the fabric and the spandex fiber. Four-way stretch fabrics do not run. Two-way stretch knits, which get their lengthwise stretch only from the spandex fiber, are thinner and snag more easily than four-way stretch knits.

Spandex is an elastic fiber often used as a core with other yarns wrapped around it.

Fabrics with two-way and four-way stretch are available in a variety of fibers combined with spandex, such as nylon/spandex, cotton/spandex, and polyester/cotton/spandex. Stretch velvet, cut velvet, stretch lace, metallic knits, and stretch illusion and net are all available with added spandex. These fabrics have 75% to 100% stretch in one direction, 35% to 50% stretch in the other direction, and great recovery.

Although all pattern companies have some patterns suitable for high-spandex knits, Kwik Sew patterns and Stretch & Sew patterns are the best choices for swimsuits and activewear because they have an excellent selection of styles and a consistent fit. Most important, these patterns take the torso length into consideration when sizing and adjusting the pattern. Torso length is an important component of getting great fit and comfort in swimsuits, leotards, and activewear.

Cutting Swimsuit Fabrics

Most swimwear fabrics have the greatest stretch in the lengthwise direction as it comes off the bolt, while cotton/spandex fabrics have the greatest stretch across the fabric, just like conventional knits. You should cut garments so the greatest stretch goes around the body when you wear the garment, and use a nap layout. To avoid snagging the fabric, use extra-fine pins or fine ballpoint pins, and confine pins to the seam allowances. Most seam allowances are ¼ in., making it necessary to cut notches going out. The seam allowance on most necklines is ⅜ in. If there is no seam at the center front and center back necklines, mark the centers with an outgoing notch or a tiny ⅛-in. snip.

Sewing Swimsuit Fabrics

Fine universal-point needles ranging in size from 9/65 to 11/75 are appropriate for most swimsuit fabrics, but if you notice any skipped stitches when sewing switch to ballpoint needles. Before sewing a garment, be sure to do a test seam.

If you are using a serger, use a three-thread serger stitch. On a sewing machine, sew seams using a stretch-overlock or double-overlock stitch placed along the edge. These stitches sew the seam and finish the edge in one step. In the process of sewing each stitch, the fabric moves back and forth, which sometimes causes the fabric edges to misalign as you sew the seam. If your fabric slips and slides, machine-baste the seam first using a ⅛-in. seam allowance to keep the edges together, then you can easily sew one of the overlock stitches along the edge.

When pinning fabrics that run or snag easily, confine pinning to the seam allowance whenever possible.

You can also sew the seams using a double-stitch combination, such as a narrow zigzag 1mm wide and 2mm long for the first stitching and a medium zigzag 2mm to 3mm wide and 2mm long or a basic machine overlock for the second stitching.

Finish the garment's neckline and edges by turning back the edge and topstitching with a medium zigzag that is 2mm to 3mm wide and long or by using multineedle straight topstitching. If you are using multineedle topstitching, use woolly nylon in the bobbin to increase the elasticity. You can also finish the neckline and edges by using self-fabric as ribbing or single-layer binding, by applying narrow binding with a binder attachment, or by inserting elastic then topstitching.

Finishing Edges with Elastic

Finishing necklines, armholes, and leg openings on swimsuits, bodysuits, and activewear with elastic keeps the edges in place, especially during vigorous activity. Necklines and edges finished with elastic have firm edges that stay put. In most cases, the elastic is meant to maintain the size of the opening rather than to reduce it. Although elasticized edges are associated with swimwear and fabrics with spandex, they are also an excellent way to stabilize all types of knits.

You should use swimsuit elastic when sewing swimsuits, but you can apply braided elastic, knitted elastic, or clear elastic in the same way to a variety of knits from sheer stretch illusion to heavy stretch chenille. Lingerie elastic helps maintain the shape and size of a neckline as well as adds a pretty picot finish to the edge. Stretch-lace trim is another elastic option that can be used to finish necklines when a firm edge is not necessary.

Preparing the garment and the elastic

The secret to smooth elastic application is to divide the elastic and the garment opening into equal sections, usually fourths. Overlap the ends of the elastic and sew them together, then using a fabric marker, divide the elastic into fourths. To divide the neckline, mark the center front and center back with a tiny ⅛-in. scissor snip, if you haven't already done so in the cutting. Match up the center front and center back neckline, and line up the neckline edges until you find the halfway points, then take short snips. (The halfway point between the center front and center back is rarely the shoulder seam. That is only the case when the front and back neckline are the same length.)

The elastic at leg openings is different. Here the elastic is inserted with a 1 to 1 ratio at the front opening, meaning no stretching, but stretched to fit the back leg opening so that it hugs the body below the derriere. You do not need to divide the leg openings into quarters.

Inserting swimsuit elastic   Swimsuit elastic has a firm hand, is treated to stand up to chlorine, and is meant to be covered by the fashion fabric.

1. *To insert the elastic, pin it to the wrong side of the neckline and armholes, lining it up to the cut edge and placing the elastic seam at the least conspicuous quarter mark, which is typically the center back, back shoulder, or underarm (see the top photo on p. 114). Match up the remaining quarter marks and pin.*
2. *With the elastic on top and the fabric facing down, start sewing at the elastic seam by using a medium zigzag or a serger stitch. Be sure to sew close to the outer edge of the elastic and the fabric (see the bottom photo on p. 114).*
3. *Fold the elastic under so that it is covered by the seam allowance.*

Pin the elastic to the wrong side of the neckline or arm-holes, matching quarter marks and placing the elastic seam at the least conspicuous quarter mark.

Using a medium zigzag stitch on a sewing machine, sew the elastic to the gar-ment edge with the elastic on top.

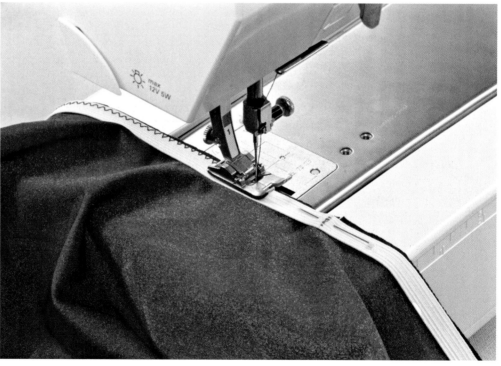

Fold the elastic under and topstitch with the right side of the garment facing up. Stretch the elastic and the fabric in front of and behind the presser foot just enough to smooth the ease. To best hold the elastic in place, use a seam allowance just slightly narrower than the width of the elastic to sew the topstitching.

4. Using a medium zigzag stitch that is 2mm to 3mm wide and long or a straight stitch with a double needle, topstitch close to the inner edge, starting at a garment seam. Stretch the elastic and fabric in front of and behind the presser foot, just enough to smooth any ease, and move with the fabric as you sew (see the photo above). It is always best to topstitch with the right side of the garment facing up. The width of the topstitching should be slightly narrower than the width of the elastic.

5. Pin the elastic to the front leg opening first, then stretch the remaining elastic to fit the remaining fabric at the back leg opening. The presser foot of your sewing machine is useful here as a third hand. Place the elastic and the leg opening under the presser foot, starting at the crotch seam or at the side seam, then stretch the leg opening and pin to distribute the ease along the back leg opening (see the photo at right).

6. Zigzag close to the outer edge, stretching the elastic just enough to flatten the ease.

On leg openings, low necklines, and places with lots of ease, pin the elastic to any matchpoints, then use the presser foot of your sewing machine as a third hand to help stretch and pin the elastic to fit the opening.

7. *Next, turn to the wrong side and topstitch close to the inner edge of the elastic, again only stretching where necessary to flatten and smooth the ease. The best stitches for topstitching elastic are a medium zigzag stitch or a twin-needle topstitch because these stitches have built-in stretch.*

Inserting lingerie elastic   Lingerie elastic is softer than swimsuit elastic and is typically stitched directly on top of the fabric, unlike swimsuit elastic that must be enclosed. This type of elastic comes in an assortment of colors and often has a picot edge. It can also be stitched in place so just the picot edge shows past the outer edge of the neckline, armhole, leg opening, or waistband that it finishes. A second type of lingerie elastic has a soft and plushy back side that is meant to be worn next to the skin and has a picot edge on one or both edges that looks pretty when it shows past the finished edge of the garment. Lingerie elastic is appropriate for lightweight single knits, stretch laces, and tricot.

To sew lingerie elastic so that just the picot edge shows at the neckline, pin the elastic on top of the right side of the garment, lining up the smooth edge of the elastic with the raw edge of the garment. Sew the elastic with a zigzag stitch near the inner, or picot, edge. To finish, fold the elastic back, and topstitch using a zigzag or triple zigzag stitch close to the inner, or smooth, edge of the elastic (see the photo below).

Inserting stretch-lace trim   Stretch-lace trim, which has a softer hand than swimsuit or lingerie elastic, can also be used to finish necklines and edges. This type of elastic is normally positioned on the outside of the neckline and topstitched in place, but you can also use it so that just a tiny bit of the lace edge shows past the neckline. Stretch-lace trim comes in different widths, but trim that is less than ¾ in. wide works best around curves. Lace trim is suitable for tricot, lightweight single knits, and stretch-lace garments.

To stitch stretch-lace trim on the outside of a neckline, pin the wrong side of the trim on top of the right side of the garment, keeping the outer edge of the lace even

To apply lingerie elastic so that just the picot edge shows at the neckline, pin the elastic on top of the right side of the neckline, lining up the smooth edge of the elastic with the cut edge. Zigzag next to the picot edge. Finish by folding back the elastic and topstitching near the inner or smooth edge.

To apply stretch-lace trim to the outside of a neckline, pin the wrong side of the stretch lace to the right side of the garment, lining up the scalloped edge with the raw edge of the garment. Using a medium zigzag, sew on the inner edge of the trim.

with the raw edge of the garment. Using a medium zigzag stitch, sew the inner edge of the lace even with the inner edge of the presser foot (see the photo above). Trim away the fabric under the lace close to the zigzag stitch.

To stitch stretch-lace trim on the inside, pin the right side of the trim to the right side of the garment, placing the scalloped edge of the trim slightly beyond the seamline. The trim will be in the seam allowance with the decorative edge extending about ¼ in. beyond the seam. Using a zigzag stitch, sew the trim in place along the seamline. To finish, fold the lace edge back along the seamline, and stitch again using a zigzag stitch close to the inner edge. Just the scalloped edge of the trim will show past the neckline.

Sewing elastic to square and V-necklines

Square and V-necks on swimwear need elastic to maintain the shape of the neckline. Often patterns with V-necklines have a center seam to facilitate installing the elastic. The following method allows you to easily elasticize square and V-necklines without needing to seam the garment.

1. Using ⅜-in. elastic, staystitch each corner or point ¼ in. from the edge, pivoting at the corner or point, then clip to the corner stitch.
2. Overlap and sew the elastic ends, then divide the elastic and the neckline into fourths and mark (see the illustration on p. 118).
3. Next, pin the elastic to the wrong side of the neckline, aligning one side of the elastic to the raw edge and matching the marks, then use a zigzag stitch to sew close to the outer edge except near the corners. At the corners, stop the zigzag stitch about ½ in. from the corner and, without interrupting the stitch, switch to a straight stitch. Use the straight stitch to sew the elastic to the corner and ½ in. past it, sewing close to the inner edge of the elastic near the staystitching. Once past the corner, return to the zigzag stitch and to the outer edge to finish sewing.

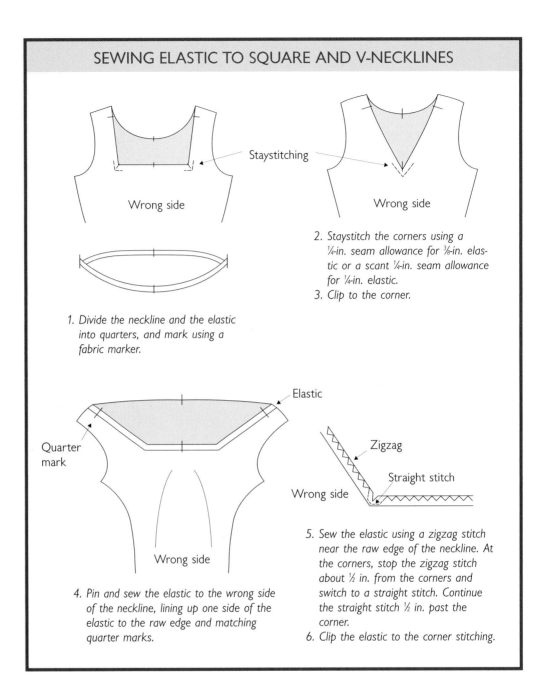

SEWING ELASTIC TO SQUARE AND V-NECKLINES

Wrong side

Staystitching

Wrong side

1. Divide the neckline and the elastic into quarters, and mark using a fabric marker.

2. Staystitch the corners using a ¼-in. seam allowance for ⅜-in. elastic or a scant ¼-in. seam allowance for ¼-in. elastic.

3. Clip to the corner.

Quarter mark

Elastic

Wrong side

Zigzag

Straight stitch

Wrong side

4. Pin and sew the elastic to the wrong side of the neckline, lining up one side of the elastic to the raw edge and matching quarter marks.

5. Sew the elastic using a zigzag stitch near the raw edge of the neckline. At the corners, stop the zigzag stitch about ½ in. from the corners and switch to a straight stitch. Continue the straight stitch ½ in. past the corner.

6. Clip the elastic to the corner stitching.

4. After stitching the elastic, replace the missing fabric and elastic at the clipped corners as is done in ready-to-wear. This must be done before turning and topstitching the neckline.

5. For each corner or point, cut a binding from the fashion fabric that is 2 in. wide by 1 in. long, having the greatest amount of stretch along the 2-in. edge.

6. On the neckline, clip the elastic at each corner to the stitching. Spread the clipped fabric edge so that the staystitching forms a straight line, and pin the longer side of the

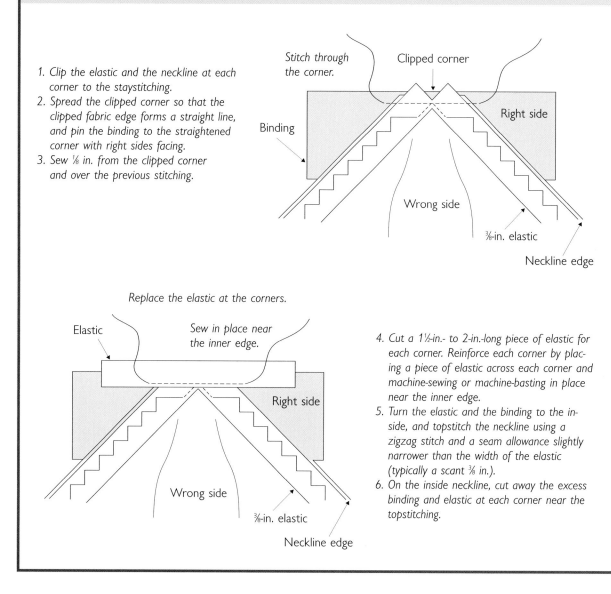

1. Clip the elastic and the neckline at each corner to the staystitching.
2. Spread the clipped corner so that the clipped fabric edge forms a straight line, and pin the binding to the straightened corner with right sides facing.
3. Sew ⅛ in. from the clipped corner and over the previous stitching.

Stitch through the corner.

Clipped corner

Right side

Binding

Wrong side

⅜-in. elastic

Neckline edge

Replace the elastic at the corners.

Elastic

Sew in place near the inner edge.

Right side

Wrong side

⅜-in. elastic

Neckline edge

4. Cut a 1½-in.- to 2-in.-long piece of elastic for each corner. Reinforce each corner by placing a piece of elastic across each corner and machine-sewing or machine-basting in place near the inner edge.
5. Turn the elastic and the binding to the inside, and topstitch the neckline using a zigzag stitch and a seam allowance slightly narrower than the width of the elastic (typically a scant ⅜ in.).
6. On the inside neckline, cut away the excess binding and elastic at each corner near the topstitching.

binding to the straightened corner with right sides together (see the illustration above). Sew the binding in place across the corner ⅛ in. from the clipped edge and over the previous stitching.

7. Cut a 1½-in.- to 2-in.-long piece of elastic for each corner. Place a strip of elastic across each corner, and machine-sew in place near the inner edge.

8. To finish the square or V-neckline, turn the elastic and binding toward the inside, and topstitch the neckline as close as possible to the inner edge of the elastic. Use a zigzag stitch to topstitch, pivoting at each corner.
9. On the inside neckline, cut away the extra binding and elastic beyond the topstitching at the corners.

Cutouts are easy to add to a swimsuit body. Oval and circular cutouts are easiest to do, but you can also do square corners following the square- or V-neckline technique for applying elastic. Use ¼-in. swimsuit elastic to help hold the shape of the new opening.

1. Try on the swimsuit inside out and mark the outline of the cutout directly on the suit using a fabric marker. Remember that the cutout will be on the opposite side when you wear the suit.

2. After taking off the suit, true the marked line so that it is smooth and balanced. If you want a centered, symmetrical cutout, mark it on the body for placement, but when you take the suit off, fold it along the center and true the cutout line, making both sides the same. The marked line is where you turn back the hem or seam allowance.

3. Next, cut the swimsuit elastic the same size as the opening. To measure, stand the elastic on one edge and line it up with the marked line.

4. Butt and sew the elastic ends, then pin the elastic to the seam allowance, lining up the edge of the elastic to the finished cutout size. Zigzag the elastic in place.

5. Cut away the swimsuit fabric next to the elastic, leaving a ¼-in. to ⅜-in. seam allowance, then turn back the elasticized hem and topstitch using a zigzag stitch.

To mark a centered, symmetrical cutout, fold along the center of the marked shape, then use a tracing wheel or dressmaker's carbon to true the other half of the cutout line.

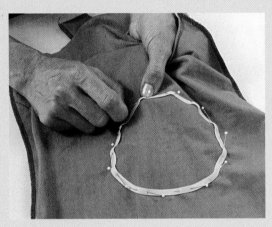

After butting and sewing the ends of the elastic together, pin and sew the elastic to the seam allowance, lining up the edge of the elastic to the marked line.

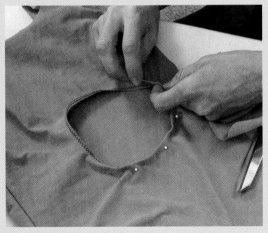

Cut away the fabric from the center of the cutout next to the elastic, then turn the elastic to the inside, pin, and topstitch about ¼ in. from the fold or near the inner edge of the elastic.

Cutting elastic for modified necklines and leg openings Part of the fun of sewing anything is to be able to modify the style or the size. Changing necklines, armholes, and leg openings is easy to do but requires changing the amount of elastic used to finish the opening. Adjusting the fit of a swimsuit can also affect the size of these openings, so it is important to gauge how much elastic to cut.

On most elastic applications, the elastic edge is meant to maintain the size of the opening, not reduce it. Therefore, cut elastic for armholes and necklines the same size as the finished edge plus ½ in. for an overlap. If the neckline is low, cut elastic 2 in. to 3 in. shorter than the neckline plus a ½-in. overlap.

For elastic at a leg opening, cut it the same size as the front leg opening plus three-quarters the measurement of the back leg opening and ½ in. for overlap. Attach the elastic to the front leg at a 1 to 1 ratio, and distribute the ease at the back leg opening along the remaining elastic.

Sewing elasticized straps Elasticized straps are sturdy, firm, and comfortable to wear. I prefer to use swimsuit elastic, but transparent elastic, which is much softer, is also an option. When making straps, first decide how wide you want them to be. Finished straps should equal the width of the elastic.

1. *Begin by cutting the fashion fabric to equal two times the width of the elastic plus ½ in. for two ¼-in. seam allowances. For example, if you are using ⅜-in. elastic, cut the fabric 1¼ in. wide. Cut the elastic 1 in.*

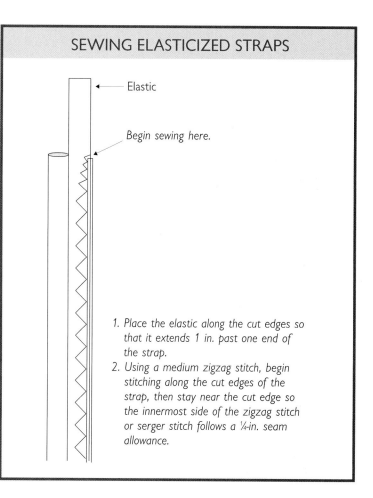

SEWING ELASTICIZED STRAPS

Elastic

Begin sewing here.

1. *Place the elastic along the cut edges so that it extends 1 in. past one end of the strap.*
2. *Using a medium zigzag stitch, begin stitching along the cut edges of the strap, then stay near the cut edge so the innermost side of the zigzag stitch or serger stitch follows a ¼-in. seam allowance.*

longer than the shoulder strap so that it extends past the strap when you sew.
2. *Pin the fashion fabric in half with right sides together, then line up one side of the elastic with the raw edges.*
3. *Using a machine zigzag or a serger, stitch through the elastic and fabric. To make it easier to turn, begin stitching along the raw edges of the seam, then sew near the cut edge so that the innermost side of the zigzag stitch or serger stitch follows a ¼-in. seam allowance (see the illustration above). Turn the strap right side out using a safety pin.*

Lining a Swimsuit or Stretch-Lace Garment

The typical reason to line a swimsuit or stretch-lace garment is to make the garment opaque or to make the fabric firmer. Base the decision to line or not line a suit on the

TIP

Clear elastic tends to stick to the serger presser foot at the start of sewing. Position the elastic so that you have 1 in. to 2 in. of elastic extending behind the presser foot at the start of each seam. This way you can pull the elastic from behind the presser foot just to get started sewing. Once you see the fabric and elastic feeding back, you can cut away the excess length.

You can easily use a serger to apply any kind of elastic to edges at a 1 to 1 ratio, meaning the elastic is the same size as the edge, without needing special attachments. To apply swimsuit, clear, braided, or knitted elastic when stabilizing necklines and edges, use a wide three-thread serger stitch and the longest stitch setting. Do not precut the elastic to the size of the opening or sew it to form a circle as you would when using a sewing machine. Start each application at the least conspicuous seam.

1. Lift the serger presser foot and the serger needle, and place the fashion fabric wrong side up under the presser foot at the starting point. Manually insert the needle into the fabric to hold it in place. With the foot still up, insert the end of the elastic until it touches the front of the needle, lining it up next to the serger knife.

2. Lower the presser foot and start sewing, being careful not to stretch the elastic or the fabric as you sew. Leave the serger knife engaged so that you can trim and neaten the edge of the fashion fabric as you sew, being sure to avoid cutting the elastic, or disengage the knife to avoid mishaps. Some sergers have a slotted opening at the front of the basic serger foot. If you have this feature, thread the elastic through the slotted opening to help guide the elastic as you sew.

3. Next, cut the elastic to size just before the starting point goes back under the serger presser foot, leaving a ¼-in. to ⅜-in. overlap. Continue sewing a bit past the overlap. The overlap will be held in place by topstitching.

4. Finally, topstitch the opening using a zigzag stitch or double needle.

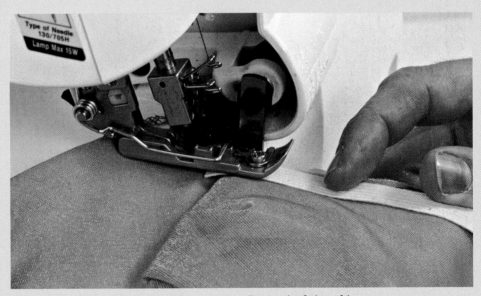

To apply elastic on a serger, lower the serger needle into the fashion fabric to hold it in place, and with the foot still up, insert the end of the elastic until it touches the front of the needle and lines up along the serger knife. Lower the presser foot and serge the elastic in place.

To apply elastic so that it gathers the fashion fabric, such as you must do on the back of leg openings, it is preferable to use an elasticator foot. An elasticator foot allows you to create a gathered edge without having to pull at the elastic, but you must do test seams to find the best setting.

Without an elasticator foot, you must stretch the elastic as you sew, and you must be careful to pull the front of the elastic just enough to fit the fashion fabric. When you apply elastic to the leg opening, the front is applied at a 1 to 1 ratio, but the back leg opening elastic must be stretched to fit.

1. Start by applying the elastic to the front leg opening following the directions on the facing page.
2. When you reach the side seam, use a ruler to measure and mark the length of the elastic for the back leg opening.

Do not cut the elastic so you will have a longer length to hold on to as you stretch the elastic at the back leg opening. The elastic should equal three-quarters the length of the back leg opening.

3. Stretch and pin the elastic to the back leg opening to evenly distribute the ease.
4. To sew the elastic in place, stretch small sections of the elastic in front of the presser foot just enough to fit the fabric, but also hold the elastic behind the presser foot taut as you sew, otherwise you can damage the loopers. Cut the elastic so that it overlaps slightly just before the starting point goes under the serger presser foot, then finish sewing the edge.
5. To sew the other leg opening, reverse the process. Start with the back leg opening where you must stretch the elastic, then finish with the front leg opening.

Cut the elastic to size just before the starting point goes back under the presser foot. Be sure to leave a ¼-in. to ⅜-in. overlap, and continue sewing for about 1 in. past the overlap.

TIP

For best results, a lining must have the same elasticity as the fashion fabric. Be sure to check both the lengthwise and crosswise stretch.

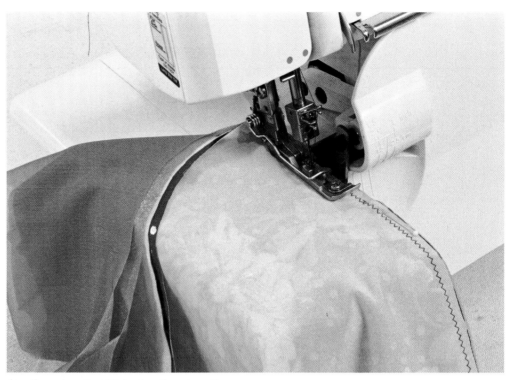

Sew the swimsuit and lining together along the center back seam.

TIP

The straight stitch pops easily if you baste the suit together and try it on, but that doesn't matter because it will eventually be caught in the permanent seam.

fashion fabric you select. It is best to either line the entire suit or not line it at all, although you see store-bought swimsuits and some swimsuit patterns with just a front lining. Lining the front only tends to pull the side seams forward and place extra stress on the unlined back.

Lined suits feel firmer than unlined ones, but if the fashion fabric is thick enough, firm enough, and opaque enough, lining is unnecessary. Lining a suit may make it feel a lot tighter than it would without a lining, depending on the firmness of both the fashion fabric and the lining fabric being used. Keep this in mind when selecting a pattern size.

Special swimsuit lining fabrics are available, but they have varying amounts of elasticity. Some are mostly nylon or poly-ester with little or no spandex, so these are suitable for small sections of a suit only, such as the bra lining or the crotch lining on an otherwise unlined suit. One option

for lining an entire garment is to use swim-suit fabric to self-line the suit. Otherwise be sure to select lining fabric that has both lengthwise and crosswise stretch just like the swimsuit fabric.

For stretch-lace garments, use a light-weight two-way stretch fabric. Stretch laces look pretty with contrasting or skin-tone linings to bring out the lace design, while a lining that matches the lace will emphasize the lace's texture.

Cutting and sewing a lining   To cut a swimsuit lining, cut the front lining the same as the suit front using the paper pat-tern, or use the lining pattern provided. If the suit back does not have a center back seam, cut the back lining using the back swimsuit pattern, and baste the lining to the back with wrong sides together. If the suit has a center back seam, cut the lining back with right sides together just like the suit back and sew as follows.

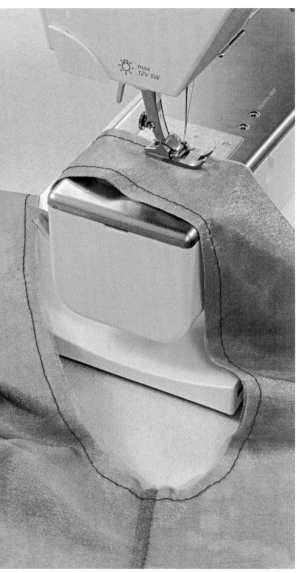

Unfold the back seam, then machine-baste the lining back to the swimsuit back with wrong sides together along the outer edges. From this point on, the back and its lining can be treated as one fabric.

center back seam with right sides together using a zigzag stitch. Then attach the lining, also with right sides together, using a second zigzag stitch or a serger.

3. Unfold the back seam, and machine-baste the wrong side of the lining to the wrong side of the swimsuit back along all the outer edges. Pattern directions typically call for a zigzag stitch for this step, but a zigzag is time-consuming and it's easier to keep the lining aligned with the fashion fabric if you use a long straight stitch.

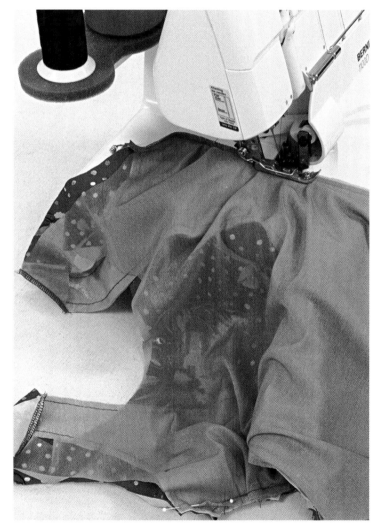

To attach the lining front, position the right side of the lining front on top of the right side of the lining back. Sew on top of the previous stitching using a serger or a second zigzag stitch.

1. With right sides facing in, place the suit back on top of the lining, also with right sides facing in.

2. Pin and sew all four layers together at the center back seam using a machine or serger overlock stitch, or double-stitch the seam. Since many high-spandex fabrics are slippery, don't hesitate to sew the center back seam in two stages. First, sew the swimsuit

The best thing about sewing swimwear and bodywear is that besides being able to perfect the fit, you can modify the style. If changing the pattern style appeals to you, then making a swimsuit sloper is invaluable.

Start with a basic pattern with a high neckline, selecting the size closest to your bust measurement. Compare the torso length or the back waist length plus crotch length for the size you are using. Make length adjustments first, copy the pattern, then change the waist and hip area if necessary. Next, cut the sloper front, back, and sleeves (depending on the style of garment you are sewing) out of cotton/spandex or nylon/spandex. Do not make any adjustments directly on the fabric without making them on the pattern.

Before basting the sloper together, attach the elastic to the neckline, leg openings, and armholes (if sleeveless) as follows. The elastic will hold the edges in place when you try on the sloper, yet you can still unstitch and adjust side and shoulder seams if necessary.

1. Cut the elastic the same size as all the openings except the back leg opening, which should be cut to three-quarters the length of the opening.
2. Place the elastic on the wrong side of the sloper, lining up the edge of the elastic to the cut edge of each opening.
3. Using a 4mm-wide and 4mm-long stitch, zigzag through the center of the elastic, and lock in the stitch at

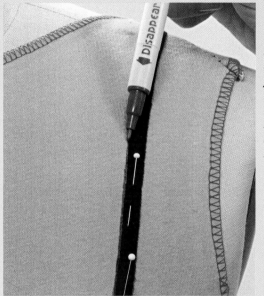

Experiment with twill tape to define new necklines or seamlines. Move and repin it until you like the placement, then mark the new neckline or seamline using a disappearing or washable marker and unpin the tape.

I typically use a disappearing marker to mark new lines on a sloper pattern, then I make a new pattern using the sloper and incorporating the new neckline or any fitting changes. This way the basic sloper pattern stays intact and ready to use again to create new style variations.

each end. To attach the elastic using a serger, use the longest and widest three-thread serger stitch.

4. Machine-baste the front to the back using a straight 5mm-long basting stitch. Leave the crotch seam open.

5. Next, try on the sloper and pin the crotch closed with a safety pin or two. Even though the basting stitches will pop when you try on the sloper, you will still be able to check the fit and draw in the style lines for your new garment.

6. Before changing the style lines, pin and mark any changes to the fit, and mark the bust point on the sloper.

7. Since there is some experimentation when marking in new necklines or seams, pin a contrasting color twill tape to the sloper where you would like to make a change. This way you can see the neckline or seam from a distance without being distracted by the extra fabric, and you can keep changing your mind until you find the perfect shape. Once you've made a decision, mark in new necklines and new style lines using a disappearing or washable marker and remove the twill tape.

8. Take off the sloper and remove the basting stitches, then transfer changes to the paper pattern using a spoked tracing wheel or marker.

9. Finally, make a new pattern by copying the sloper pattern and incorporating the changes, being sure to add seam allowances where necessary.

To reduce bulk if the fabric is thick, machine-baste the lining to the neckline, armholes, and leg openings using a seam allowance equal to the width of the elastic (normally ⅜ in.). This way you can trim away the lining from the seam allowances before attaching the elastic.

4. Next, sew the unlined swimsuit front to the lined swimsuit back at the side seams, shoulder seams, and crotch seam with right sides together. Do this on a sewing machine using a zigzag stitch that is 1mm wide and 2mm long.

5. Pin the lining front to the suit front at the side seams, shoulder seams, and crotch seam with right sides together. Position the right side of the lining front on top of the right side of the lining back, then sew on top of the previous stitch using a three-thread serger stitch or a medium zigzag stitch.

6. Turn the garment right side out so the suit and lining are wrong sides together.

7. Finally, pin and baste the remaining edges of the front lining to the suit and treat as one layer to attach the elastic.

Using an underlining as a swimsuit lining

This lining method is really an underlining method because you connect the lining to the individual swimsuit pieces before sewing the seams and the seams are left exposed. Underlining is typically used to line stretch lace to avoid having the seams show on the outside, but you also can use it as a simple way to line a suit.

To underline a swimsuit, cut the lining the same as the suit, then baste the wrong side of the lining to the wrong side of the suit using a long straight stitch and sewing ⅛ in. from the edge. Now treat as one layer as you sew the garment and finish the edges.

STRETCH VELVETS, CHENILLE, TERRY, AND OTHER NAPPED KNITS

Napped pile knits such as stretch velvets, velour, stretch chenille, stretch suede cloth, and stretch terry have the luxurious look of their woven counterparts combined with the ease and comfort associated with sewing and wearing knitted fabrics.

Using a napped fabric makes a plain pattern special and more interesting so you don't have to make an effort to select a complex style. Select patterns with simple shapes and few seams until you get used to cutting and sewing a napped pile surface. Napped fabrics are appropriate for most knitted patterns as long as they have the right amount of stretch. Patterns that are not compatible with napped fabrics will state that on the envelope. If you use a pattern meant for wovens, keep the style simple and take the amount of stretch in the fabric into consideration when you choose the size and the silhouette.

Napped pile knits shade more dramatically than basic, flat knits so you will have to figure out which color you prefer. The color of the fabric looks lighter and has a surface sheen when cutting so that the nap is smooth as it runs down the garment, while cutting so the nap is smooth as it runs up the garment results in a darker, more intense color and a matte finish.

Seeing the two shades side by side makes it easier to find your preference. Do this by draping the length of fabric around the back of your neck so that when you look in the mirror, you will have the nap running down on one side and running up on the other. Depending on the color and type of napped fabric you are using, the color differences will range from subtle to dramatic. Once you decide which direction you prefer, draw arrows on the wrong side of the fabric near a lengthwise edge pointing to the end you prefer to have going up when you wear the garment.

Decide if you like a fabric better with the smooth direction of the pile running up or down the garment. Depending on the color and texture of the fabric you are using, the color differences may be subtle or dramatic.

TIP
When sewing skirts or pants that are to be worn with an overblouse or tunic, remember that napped fabrics tend to grab on to anything that is layered over them. For example, a pair of leggings with the smooth nap running up has a tendency to push a tunic up because the nap is smoother in that direction. Cutting the leggings so that the nap is running down has the opposite effect.

Cutting Napped Pile Knits

To cut napped knits, place all the pattern pieces so the upper edges are going in the direction of the arrows you have drawn. The printed names of the pattern pieces can help you identify the upper edge on more abstract pieces. Be sure the printed names are facing in the same direction on the layout.

You can expect napped fabrics to shift during cutting and sewing. To control shifting when cutting, fold the fabric lengthwise with the napped sides out, or better still, lay out a single layer of fabric with the napped side down. Just remember to turn each pattern piece over when you cut the remaining side. Pin within the seam allowances whenever possible.

If the pattern you are using has ¼-in. seam allowances, be sure to increase the seam allowances on all napped knits to ½ in. or ⅜ in. to better control the seams when you sew the garment. The larger

seams are more forgiving if a little shifting occurs when you sew the seams, are easier to sew if the fabric curls at the edges, and are compatible with using a walking foot. Increase hem allowances to 1 in. or 1¼ in. on fabrics that curl at the edges so the hem will stay smooth.

Sewing Napped Pile Knits

Napped fabrics have a tendency to shift and creep during sewing, but if you take precautions, you can minimize the effect. Compared with using a standard foot, a walking foot makes sewing effortless because it feeds the top layer of fabric at the same rate as the bottom layer.

If you are using a standard presser foot and have a knee lever, use the knee lever to lift the presser foot just enough to smooth the top layer of fabric toward the foot whenever the fabric starts to creep forward as you sew the seam. Be sure the needle is in the cloth before lifting the presser foot,

When laying out pattern pieces on napped fabric, place all pieces so that the upper edges are going in the direction you have selected.

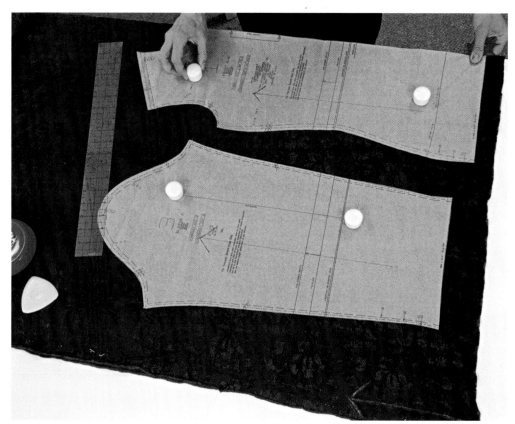

Whenever the top layer of fabric starts to creep forward, be sure the needle is in the fabric, then lift the presser foot and smooth the top layer toward the needle.

either by manually inserting the needle in the cloth or by using the needle-down feature on the sewing machine. Pinning at frequent intervals and stitching seams following the smooth direction of the nap also help to control shifting of the layers.

Pressing Napped Knits

Although knitted fabrics don't require much pressing, some is inevitable. You should test the fabric that you are sewing, keeping in mind that all napped pile fabrics, especially velvets, are not the same, even if they have the same appearance. Using your scraps, overpress them to see what damage is possible so that you avoid this in the garment. Also check to see if overpressing can be corrected by washing the sample. Variations in the density of a knit and the types of fibers used affect its resiliency.

Using a steam iron, you should do as much pressing as possible from the wrong side, placing the fashion fabric face down on top of a Velva board or a layer of plain velour or velvet fabric. You can also use the velvet fabric as a press cloth to press the

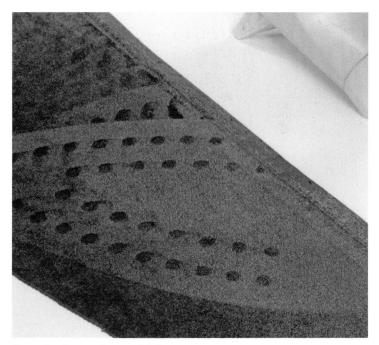

By testing iron settings on fabric scraps, you can find out what damage is possible and learn to avoid it.

To apply interfacing to facings, place a velvet press cloth pile side up on the ironing board, then place the fashion fabric face down on the cloth. Fuse the interfacing by using a standard press cloth on top of it.

Interfacing Napped Pile Knits

In spite of the pressing limitations, it is still possible to use fusible interfacings on most napped fabrics. You can fuse interfacing to most fabrics without applying a lot of pressure. Nonwoven fusible interfacing is fine for small neck facings, and tricot interfacings such as Fusi Knit, Sof Brush, and So Sheer work very nicely. On cut velvets, which tend to have a lightweight, semisheer base fabric, I find So Sheer to be very useful for interfacing. You should apply interfacing to facings only, and always use a velvet press cloth with the napped side up to cover the ironing board. Place the fashion fabric to be interfaced face down, and fuse the interfacing using a standard press cloth as a barrier.

Sewing Stretch Velvets, Cut Velvets, and Stretch Suede Cloth

When sewing seams on stretch velvets, cut velvets, and stretch suede cloth on a sewing machine, a walking foot easily controls lengthwise shifting, but one layer of the fabric may shift to the left or right of the presser foot, causing the edges to misalign. You can control or prevent this sideways shifting movement by holding the fabric to the left of the foot and pressing the layers of fabric down to the machine surface with your fingers as you sew the seams.

Keeping the seam allowances together, sew the seams using a narrow zigzag stitch for the first stitch and a medium to wide zigzag for the second stitch. You can also use a double-overlock stitch placed along the ⅝-in. seamline. In both cases, trim the seam allowance next to the outer stitching line after sewing the seams.

On a serger, use a three- or four-thread serger stitch, and adjust the differential feed to eliminate stretching the seams. Once again, pressing the fabric layers down to the machine surface to the left of the presser foot with your fingers helps keep the cut edges from shifting as you sew. Stabilize the shoulder seams using clear elastic or bias tricot.

right side of the garment. In all cases, avoid adding any pressure by holding the iron over the pressing surface without pressing down. Let the steam do the work. On more delicate fabrics, eliminate any weight, using the iron to touch the surface but keeping the contact to the fabric light.

You can prevent the sideways shifting that can happen when sewing napped fabrics by holding the fabric to the left of the presser foot and pressing the layers down to the machine surface as you sew.

Stretch velvet and velour are probably my favorite fabrics to use for appliqué because of their dramatic effect and luxurious texture. Since most of these velvets are washable and dry-cleanable, you can appliqué on all sorts of base fabrics to create casual, sophisticated, or elegant styles with equal ease. Stretch velvets and velours are also much more resilient than woven velvets, which makes them practical to use for embellishment.

The best time to add appliqué to a garment is at the beginning of construction because the flatter the design surface, the easier it is to sew. However, sometimes there is a bit of experimentation that must go on to arrive at a final design. To decide on the placement of a design, sew the shoulder seams and place the garment on a dress form or on yourself. If the design extends into the sleeve area, you can even install the sleeves into the armscyes. If necessary, temporarily pin or baste the side seams closed so that you can accurately check the placement.

To prepare the stretch velvet or velour you plan to use for your appliqué, fuse interfacing to the back of it to control shedding and to stabilize it. I prefer to keep the appliqués as soft as possible because even though stiff appliqués are easier to sew, they are not flattering to wear.

The easiest way to hold an appliqué in place while you sew is to create iron-on appliqués using Wonder Under. Wonder Under is a two-step adhesive backing that you fuse to the wrong side of the fabric that you wish to make

Once you have positioned appliqués on a garment in a pleasing design, iron them in place if you have used Wonder Under, or use spray adhesive.

fusible. First, fuse Wonder Under to the interfaced stretch velvet following the product directions, then peel away the paper backing and cut out your appliqué shapes. Position the appliqués on the garment to decide on the placement, then iron the appliqués in place using a velvet press cloth.

Sometimes it is necessary to press from the back side of the garment as well. In that case, place the garment face down on a velvet press cloth and press again. If you don't want to use Wonder Under to hold the appliqué in place while you sew, use spray adhesive on the back of the interfaced appliqué.

The advantage to using knitted appliqués on knitted fabrics is that the edges of the appliqués do not fray easily, so a simple zigzag stitch is enough to hold the edges in place. This is a good thing when

you are trying to keep things soft because the edges of the appliqué won't distort as they would if you were using a satin stitch without stabilizer to support it. You can also use some of the decorative stitches on your machine to hold the edges of the appliqué, but you may need to increase the stitch length to avoid having too solid a border of stitches when you are trying to keep things soft.

Before sewing the appliqué, do a test sample to make sure that you like the stitch and to see if additional stabilizer is needed. Normally, interfacing the appliqué is sufficient, but knits, especially sweaterknits, have a spongy texture that may require a little extra help feeding through the machine. Knits tend to linger in the same place too long and get stuck or build up stitches in the same place.

If the fabric has trouble feeding, use water-soluble stabilizer or a piece of crisp paper underneath the garment to improve the feeding action of the machine. Increasing the stitch length also helps. If paper is not enough, I lightly fuse interfacing to the back side of the appliqué area, then remove as much as possible by cutting it away next to the stitching at the end. I don't recommend using tear-away stabilizer because the type of stitch being used is not dense enough to enable the material to easily tear way.

Another way to stabilize the appliqué area is to place a layer of organza underneath the fashion fabric and cut away the excess after stitching the appliqués. To hold the organza in place, use an embroidery hoop. Select the largest hoop that will allow a full range of movement on your sewing machine, which is about 8 in. on most home machines. An embroidery hoop is a terrific aid because framing the fabric also stabilizes the appliqué area.

To sew the appliqué, start on a side that follows the nap because sewing in the direction that smoothes the nap is also smoother to sew. Use a machine embroidery foot and a medium to wide zigzag depending on the fabrics that you are combining. For example, on my sample sweaterknit, I used a 3.5mm stitch width and a 2mm stitch length. The stitch length on the garment looks more like 1.5mm because of the soft, spongy, and thick texture of the sweaterknit and the limited amount of stabilizer that was used.

If the fabric has trouble feeding because of its bulk or texture, use stabilizer or a crisp piece of paper underneath the garment to improve the feeding action.

A walking foot is especially useful on bulky napped-pile knits such as stretch chenille.

Sewing Stretch Chenille

Chenille knits are luxurious and bulky. To sew them, a walking foot is very useful. When sewing seams using a standard presser foot, help the top layer feed under the presser foot by pushing it toward the foot. Take rest stops, and with the needle down, lift the presser foot and smooth the top layer toward the foot.

Sew seams using double-stitched seams. A narrow zigzag 1mm wide and 2.5mm long works for the first stitching. For the second stitching, sew a zigzag next to the first using a 2mm stitch length and a 3mm, 4mm, or 5mm stitch width, depending on the density of the stitch and the fabric thickness. If the test seam is stretched out of shape, increase the stitch length. Otherwise use a double-overlock or stretch-overlock stitch along the ⅝-in. seamline rather than along the edge and trim away the excess seam after stitching.

Because chenille knits are typically loosely knitted and heavy, I like to use a serger stitch in addition to a narrow zigzag stitch. On bulky knits, using a four-thread serger stitch is useful because it creates a wider and more stable seam than a three-thread stitch. Alternatively, use a three-thread stitch with the left needle to sew the widest possible three-thread stitch. Adjust the differential feed to reduce stretching in the seams.

Necklines and edges can be finished with a turned-and-stitched edge, ribbing, binding, or possibly facings, depending on the style, thickness of the fabric, and the amount of stretch. Because most chenille knits are heavy, turned-and-stitched necklines tend to stretch out of shape, so stabilize the edge using clear elastic before turning back and topstitching. To stabilize, cut the clear elastic the same size as the neckline, then sew the ends together to form a circle. Divide the neckline and the elastic into fourths, then sew the elastic to the wrong side of the neckline (see

Finish necklines and edges using shaped facings, single-layer bindings, ribbing, or by turning back and topstitching. Always do a test sample, and adjust your method to solve any problems. If a turned-back-and-topstitched neckline stretches out, sew clear elastic to the wrong side of the neckline using a medium zigzag stitch. Cut the elastic the same size as the neckline, and follow the directions for applying elastic on pp. 113-121, or use the flat method to apply clear elastic on a serger.

To sew hems, use single-, double-, or triple-needle topstitching for the best results. Alternatively, you can topstitch using a medium zigzag stitch that is 2mm to 3mm wide and long. Sew hems invisibly by hand with a blind catchstitch, by machine using a 2mm wide and long zigzag stitch with a blind-hem foot, or by serging using a blind hem on thick velours and velvets that have lots of texture. Using a false blind hem on a serger produces a banded effect.

TIP

When using chenille, be sure to stabilize the shoulder seams using Seams Great or clear elastic.

pp. 113-121.) To attach the elastic on a serger, see pp. 122-123.

Another way to create a very strong edge is to use a binder attachment and binding made from lightweight jersey or tricot cut on the crossgrain or a bias-cut woven fabric. You can use the narrow bound edge as the finished edge, or turn it to the inside of the garment and topstitch the garment edge to hold the binding in place.

Hem chenille invisibly by hand using a blind catchstitch or by using a blind-hemming stitch on a machine or serger. To blind-hem stitch by machine, use a blind-hem foot and a zigzag stitch, setting the stitch width to 2mm and the stitch length to 5mm. Topstitch hems and edges using a medium zigzag 3mm wide and 3mm long or more, depending on the thickness of the fabric.

When using narrow binding and a binder attachment to finish an edge, the binding can be the finished edge on the outside of the garment (top), or it can be turned to the inside of the garment and top-stitched with a straight stitch or zigzag to hold it in place (bottom). In both cases, be sure to use a thin fabric for the binding.

Sewing Stretch Terry

Stretch terries have a looped pile surface on one side and a smooth, plain stitch on the other. When cutting stretch terry, use ½-in. or ⅝-in. seam allowances. To sew on a sewing machine, use an overlock or stretch-overlock stitch placed on the seamline, then trim away the seam allowance next to the stitching line. A walking foot is useful if the stretch terry is thick. You can also use double-stitched seams to sew the garment. A narrow zigzag 1mm wide and 2.5mm long for the first stitching and a medium to wide zigzag 2mm to 3mm wide and long for the second stitching work well. Another seam option is to press seams to one side, then topstitch in place using single- or double-needle topstitching.

A stretch-overlock stitch is useful for sewing flat, overlapped seams instead of standard seams to keep bulk to a minimum. Otherwise, you can sew these seams on a serger using a four-thread serger stitch or using a three-thread serger stitch with the left needle to create wider seams. Adjust the differential feed to reduce stretching in the seams.

To topstitch hems, use single- or double-needle topstitching. Sew a blind hem on a sewing machine using a blind-hem foot and a 2mm-wide and 5mm-long zigzag stitch or on a serger using a blind-hemming stitch. Finish necklines and edges by turning back and topstitching or by using shaped facings, binding, or ribbing. Use a stretch-overlock stitch or twin-needle topstitching to sew facing edges to the outer garment so that they always stay in place.

SYNTHETIC FLEECE

Synthetic fleece is a high-tech, high-loft fleece fabric that is very warm, very lightweight, and durable. It was originally developed and used for cold-weather gear and active outerwear, but you don't have to be the outdoor type to appreciate and enjoy wearing this attractive and practical fabric.

Synthetic fleece fabrics are typically stable knits with little to moderate cross-wise stretch and almost no lengthwise stretch. Fleece with added spandex has more stretch in both directions. Unlike most bulky fabrics, the cut edges don't unravel because under all the fluff is a fine, dense, knitted fabric so the seams stay neat. Because of these qualities, fleece is easy to cut and sew, and all sorts of possibilities for simplifying construction are opened up. Techniques like overlapped seams and decorative appliqué are easy to do because you don't have to turn back the edges.

Patterns designed with synthetic fleece in mind are easy to find due to the fabric's popularity. Expect to find the standard fleece styles that you find in store-bought clothes, such as sporty zipper-front jackets or vests, straight or blouson pullover styles that you associate with casual sportswear, as well as some craft-inspired jackets. For more interesting style alternatives, look at patterns meant for other fabrics, keeping in mind that the style doesn't have to be sporty if you are not the sporty type. Patterns meant for other fabrics can be easily adapted, but don't expect flat, crisp edges when using synthetic fleece.

Bulk needs to be considered when choosing a pattern. Depending on the weight and thickness of the fleece you are using, standard facings may equal very bulky edges. Stack up four layers of the fleece to find out how thick it will get when you overlap the front edges of the garment, and remember this doesn't include the seam allowance. If you want to keep the facings but reduce some bulk, use a lightweight fleece, sweatshirt fleece, jersey, or interlock as the facing fabric. A zipper closure reduces bulk at the front edge because there is no overlap, while single-layer collars or collars with bound edges reduce bulk at the neckline.

Fleece is machine washable, but in order to maintain the loft of the fabric, avoid pressing as you sew. Instead, finger-press and pin to hold edges and hems in place. If interfacing is necessary, you can sometimes use fusible interfacing as long as you are careful not to apply pressure and if you add the interfacing to the facing layers only. This way if the pile gets flattened, it will be on the inside of the garment. Do a test sample to determine how the interfacing will fuse and to see if you like the results. Keep in mind that light fusing that just holds the interfacing in place may be enough, and it is easier and faster than using sew-in interfacing.

Do a test sample to determine how interfacing will fuse to fleece and to see if you like the results.

Cutting Synthetic Fleece

Fleece is stable and easy to cut. When cutting, be sure to use a napped layout. Long, glass-headed pins such as quilting pins are very useful on these bulky fabrics. Because of the thickness of the fabric, trim the pattern first to avoid tearing the edges when you cut, whether you use a rotary cutter or scissors to do the cutting. Be aware of how you angle the blades of the scissors or rotary cutter when you cut because you could end up beveling the edge and cutting two different-sized layers. On thick fleeces, cutting one layer at a time is always more accurate.

Because synthetic fleece does not fray easily, it can be cut with ¼-in., ½-in., or ⅝-in. seam allowances. How you plan to finish the seams can help you decide which seam allowance is best to use. For example, if you plan to keep the seams together and sew on a sewing machine with a straight stitch plus a zigzag or any of the overlock stitches, it is easier and faster to cut the garment with ¼-in. seam allowances. If you plan to topstitch the seams open, use mock flat-felled seams, or sew the seams on a serger, use a ½-in. or ⅝-in. seam allowance.

Sewing Synthetic Fleece

When sewing seams, use a size 80 universal-point needle and 100% polyester thread. All of the sewing-machine overlock stitches produce very neat, single-process seams on this fabric. Use a machine overlock, double-overlock, or stretch-overlock stitch along the cut edge of a seam using a 5mm stitch width and a 2mm stitch length. Sew double-stitched seams using a narrow zigzag stitch 0.5mm to 1.5mm wide and 2.5mm long for the first stitching and a medium to wide zigzag 2mm to 5mm wide and 3mm long for the second stitching. Another seam option is to use a mock flat-felled seam (see pp. 41-42).

If you are sewing seams on a sewing machine, help the fabric feed by squeezing the fabric layers together just before they feed under the presser foot. If your sewing machine has the option, reduce the pressure of the presser foot. Otherwise you can use a walking foot, but the seam allowance must be at least ½ in. wide for there to be enough contact with the fabric.

TIP

I find that pinning to just the top layer of fleece cuts down on the waves created by pinning through both layers of thick fabric.

TIP

For patch pockets on fleece garments, remove the side and bottom seam allowances, but leave the opening hem in place to maintain the shape of the opening.

If you are using a serger, sew seams using a wide three- or four-thread serger stitch, and increase the differential feed as necessary to control stretching the seam. Flatlock seams sewn on a serger are very flat, butted seams that are attractive on both sides and are useful when sewing reversible fabrics.

To finish necklines and edges, turn back and topstitch with a single- or multiple-needle straight stitch or a medium to wide zigzag stitch, or by using shaped facings, single binding, double binding, or ribbing. Keep the thickness of the fleece you are using in mind when selecting a neckline finish.

If your garment fabric is very bulky, use other fabrics for bindings and facings. Look for trim fabrics that are compatible with the fleece, such as polyester, nylon, jersey,

interlock, and ribbing fabrics. Swimsuit fabrics with spandex are also good trim choices. Be aware that cotton trim fabrics may not be the best choices because they absorb moisture and take much longer to dry than fleece fabrics. If the garment is not going to be used for active outdoor activity where getting wet and staying warm are issues, the compatibility of the trim fabric is not as important. If you plan to use elastic, the casing applications on pp. 63-69 are suitable for synthetic fleece.

Hems can be finished invisibly on a sewing machine using a blind-hem foot with a zigzag stitch 2mm wide and 2mm to 5mm long. You can also topstitch using a single or multiple needle or decorative stitches. On a serger, use either a blind-hemming, a mock blind-hemming, or a flatlock-hemming stitch.

Additional Seam and Edge Finishes

Fleece is a fabric you can have fun sewing. Because the cut edges don't unravel, you can sew a garment using lapped seams, pinked or fringed edges, decorative machine stitches, and appliquéd printed borders instead of conventional edge finishes. This subject has been thoroughly covered in other books specializing in sewing synthetic fleece, but I encourage you to experiment with using the embroidery or utility stitches of your sewing machine to appliqué interesting border prints as I did on the fleece scarf shown on p. 138.

SLINKY KNITS, MATTE JERSEY, AND NOVELTY KNITS

Slinky knits, matte jersey, knitted lamé, and other novelty knits have a fluid drape that is flattering to all figure types if you choose the right pattern. Those with moderate stretch or better are the most versatile because you can sew a wide range of styles from the same fabric, from a very close-fitting T-shirt or bodysuit to a flowing tunic, dress, skirt, or full, fluid pants.

It's natural to think that slinky knits are just for slinky bodies, but you can create flattering, loose-fitting styles that flow over the body and move as you move because these knits have a weight and drape similar to silk. For best results, select styles with simple shapes and ample ease that will flow over your figure, or if you prefer close-fitting styles that follow the body, choose ones without complicated seams or tailoring.

You can expect to find a variety of pattern styles that are suitable for these fabrics, from easy pull-on dresses and separates to more complex designer patterns. Basic knitwear shapes look dressed up in these fabrics, so the style doesn't have to be complicated. It's often possible to use patterns meant for wovens, but you must consider the amount of stretch in the fabric when looking at the design elements. If your fabric has a great disparity between crosswise and length-

wise stretch and the pattern is cut on the bias, the crosswise grain will eventually stretch more than the lengthwise grain, creating unwanted asymmetry. Matte jersey fabrics tend to be more stable, so they are more conducive to being used with standard sewing techniques than are slinky knits.

Cutting Slinky Knits, Matte Jersey, and Novelty Knits

Because the weight of these fabrics puts extra stress on the upper garment seams, particularly when sewing dresses and other long garments, be sure to cut the fabric so that any runs would come up from the hem of the garment. Pulling across the grain along both cut edges of a knitted fabric will tell you if the fabric runs easily and in which direction it will run. When you lay out the fabric, be careful not to let it hang past the edge of the cutting table since this will stretch it crosswise or lengthwise.

When you lay out slinky knits and matte jersey, be careful not to let any part of it hang past the cutting table. It will stretch out of shape and probably slide off the table altogether.

TIP

Garments made from fluid and slippery knits, especially large items such as dresses, pants, tunics, and long skirts, should be stored flat to maintain their original shapes.

Fluid and slippery knits are easier to sew if you cut ½-in. or ⅝-in. seam allowances, then trim the seam allowance after machine sewing or during serging. The larger seam allowance is less likely to stretch out as you sew, and you can better control or guide the fabric under the presser foot or serger foot. You will sew better seams if you pin long seams on your work-table rather than on your lap. Using a worktable makes it easier to distribute the fabric evenly and smoothly and contributes to smooth seams.

Sewing Slinky Knits

Slinky knits have luminous colors and exciting finishes, all variations of the basic acetate and spandex finely ribbed fabric. Select patterns with simple lines and few seams, and avoid crosswise seam details that would stretch out the ribbing. Like the other fabrics in this section, the silhouette can be very close fitting or generously cut and drapey. Because slinky knits are ribbed knits, they make excellent self-trim. You can use the techniques that apply to ribbed knits on slinky knits (see pp. 94-97).

Slinky knits have texture, thickness, and lengthwise stretch that all increase its tendency to stretch easily. For more control, cut garments using a ½-in. or ⅝-in.

seam allowance, and sew seams using a double-stitched seam combination. Use a narrow to medium zigzag with a 1mm to 2mm stitch width and a 2.5mm stitch length for the first stitching, then a wider and longer zigzag for the second stitching, and trim the seam allowance.

Alternatively, you can trim the seam allowance to ¼ in. after sewing the narrow zigzag along the seamline, then use a machine overlock stitch with an over-the-edge foot, increasing the stitch length as necessary to avoid stretching. A machine overlock may be used as an alternative to the first and second stitching if the slinky knit is more stable, or as an alternative to the second stitching if you have trouble controlling the seam.

When using the double-overlock or the stretch-overlock stitch to sew and finish the seam, place the overlock stitch on the seamline, and trim away the excess seam allowance after sewing the seam. If you have a serger, use a three-thread serger stitch to sew the seam, or use it as the second row of stitching combined with a narrow zigzag stitch. If necessary, increase the differential feed to reduce stretching the seam. Be sure to stabilize shoulder seams using bias tricot or clear elastic (see pp. 70-73).

Some slinky knits have enough resilience to use the turned-back-and-topstitched method you see on the necklines and edges of store-bought garments. The firmness and the amount of spandex of the knitted fabric, the density of the stitch, and the size and weight of the total garment are factors that determine how well an edge maintains its shape. You should do a test seam.

If a garment is large and heavy, you can help maintain the shape of necklines and armholes by using clear elastic or braided elastic (see pp. 113-121). Single-layer binding and narrow binding made using a binder attachment make nice neckline finishes (see pp. 52-53). You can also use self-fabric as ribbing (see pp. 56-58). All of the elastic waistband applications described on pp. 63-69 are appropriate for slinky knits. Choose the most suitable method based on the amount of ease at the garment waistline and whether or not you want to have visible topstitching at the waistline.

To finish hems, use twin-needle topstitching or a medium to wide zigzag, depending on the thickness of the fabric. Use the medium zigzag on thin fabrics, and increase the width and length of the zigzag if the fabric is thick. It is best to use close-together needles to avoid a raised effect between the two rows of stitches. Using woolly nylon thread in the bobbin and loosening the needle tension also help flatten the ridge.

TIP

If stitches pop, you need to increase the elasticity of the seam by increasing the stitch width and decreasing the stitch length.

Sewing Matte Jersey

Designers love to use matte jersey because its elegant matte finish, its weight, and its drape make it conducive to sewing both simple garments and sophisticated styles like draped and complex evening dresses.

Matte jersey requires special care. Rayon matte jersey must be dry-cleaned because it shrinks considerably when you wash it, and sometimes the texture changes as well. You should preshrink rayon the same way as other dry-clean-only knits (see p. 30). Otherwise, have your dry cleaner put the fabric through a cleaning cycle (instead of just having it steamed) because careless steaming is more likely to stretch out your knitted fabric yardage.

Polyester matte jersey is washable and not as heavy as rayon, but it still has a nice drape and is easier to care for than the rayon or silk variety. Silk matte jersey is typically labeled dry-clean only, but some can be hand-washed, so experiment with a swatch.

More stable matte jersey may be cut with narrow seam allowances and then machine- or serger-overlocked along the edge, otherwise use ½-in. or ⅝-in. seam allowances. In most cases, you can sew using a universal-point needle in a size ranging between 9/65 to 11/75, but if you get skipped stitches or if the knitted fabric is delicate and runs easily, switch to a fine ballpoint needle.

You can sew simple garments using a three- or four-thread serger stitch or one of the overlock stitches on a sewing machine placed along the seamline. Trim the excess seam allowance after you machine-overlock the seam. On very thin matte jersey, a baby serger stitch works best. As for thread, using woolly nylon in the upper looper or in both the upper and lower loopers creates a soft, elastic seam. If you are getting stretched seams, increase the setting of the differential feed.

On complex styles, you will have more control and get better results by sewing first on a sewing machine, then using a second, wider stitch or a serger to finish the edges.

Use a narrow to medium zigzag that is 0.5mm to 2mm wide and 2mm long for the first stitching and a medium zigzag, a machine-overlock stitch, or a three-thread serger stitch for the second stitching. Increasing the width of the first stitching increases elasticity in the seam, which may be necessary if the matte jersey has some spandex and is therefore more elastic in both width and length. A machine-stretch stitch is a good first stitch for lengthwise seams on fabrics with minimal or no lengthwise stretch, such as 100% polyester matte jersey, which is fairly stable but still needs stretchy seams because of the weight of the fabric.

Shoulder seams should be stabilized using bias tricot or clear elastic (see pp. 70-73). Finish necklines by turning back and topstitching or by using shaped facings, single-layer binding, narrow binding applied with a binder attachment, or self-fabric ribbing. Elasticized edges work nicely here. If turning back and topstitching the edge stretches out the neckline, use clear elastic applied the same way as for elasticized edges. Use braided elastic to stabilize necklines on large garments made from heavy matte jersey fabrics.

Another simple way to finish necklines and edges is by using straight facings or purchased single-fold bias tape using the techniques described on pp. 59-63. All of the elastic waistband applications described on pp. 63-69 are suitable for matte jersey, especially the invisible waistband treatments. Select the elastic application that is most compatible with the amount of ease in the waist of the garment.

To finish hems, use single- or multiple-needle topstitching. When using a single row of topstitching to hem close-fitting garments, use a medium zigzag setting of 2mm to 3mm for the stitch width and length. If the fabric does not curl, a narrow hem allowance is fine, otherwise use a 1-in. hem allowance.

If you are hemming by hand, use a blind catchstitch. The blind-hemming stitch on a serger or a sewing machine shows up too much for my taste, but I like the more intentional look of the false blind hem on a serger: It looks like an add-on band of fabric. Scalloped edges, picot edges, and lettuce edges are other possible hem finishes suitable for lightweight fabrics with lots of stretch.

It is common to see matte jersey garments lined to the edge using a lighter-weight but similar knitted fabric such as very lightweight interlock, jersey, or tricot. If you are adding a lining, be sure to stabilize the neckline and the armhole edges on sleeveless garments using clear elastic as described on pp. 145-147.

Sewing Novelty Knits

Novelty knits that are fluid and drapey, such as knitted lamé, are an important part of this category of fabrics. Some knitted lamé fabrics have a metallic coating over jersey or fine interlock fabric and look like

liquid metal, while other variations have metallic yarns that create a flecked effect. The background fabric may be opaque or semisheer. Another variation has a low-profile, silky, looped surface and is available in prints and in solid colors. For these fabrics, use the techniques described for matte jersey.

Stabilizing Slinky Knits, Matte Jersey, and Novelty Knits

When you decide to sew conventional styles in matte jersey and similar novelty knits with facings, linings, and zippers, you will need to know how to stabilize these areas while maintaining the soft effect you expect from these drapey fabrics. Here is how to stabilize seams and necklines without using interfacing.

Stabilizing crosswise and diagonal seams

Crosswise and diagonal seams have a tendency to stretch easily, so they must be stabilized for professional results. The objective is to create seams and edges that hold their shape but still have some degree of stretch.

If a pattern calls for using knitted fabrics, the directions may instruct you on how to stabilize the seams, but since there are so many different knits, the technique could be inappropriate for your fabric. For example, my dress pattern calls for using fabric with two-way stretch and stabilizing the diagonal seams connecting the bodice to the skirt by centering Stay Tape over the seamline. Stay Tape is a wonderful product for stabilizing anything that you don't want to stretch, but it's a bad idea here because it won't work with such a stretchy fabric. Centering the Stay Tape on the seam restricts the fabric, creating a bulky seam that won't stretch at all. Instead, I stabilized the seams using clear elastic.

To create stable yet elastic seams that can support the weight of the fabric, use clear elastic placed in the seam allowance and next to the seamline instead of centering it on the seam.

1. Cut the elastic the same length as the seam, then zigzag in place in the seam allowance and next to the seamline on the wrong side of the fabric. Use a medium zigzag stitch that is 2mm to 3mm wide and long.

To align clear elastic with a ⅝-in. seamline, position the elastic between the toes of the presser foot, then place the wrong side of the seam allowance under the elastic so that the left edge of the elastic is ⅝ in. from the fabric edge. See what line you need to follow on your machine to keep this placement.

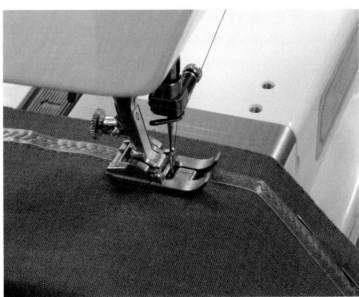

When you sew the seam, use a narrow zigzag next to the elastic.

After stabilizing soft or draped necklines that are faced or lined using clear elastic, trim the facing seam allowance to ¼ in., which is next to the elastic. Then finger-press the seam allowance toward the facing to prepare to understitch.

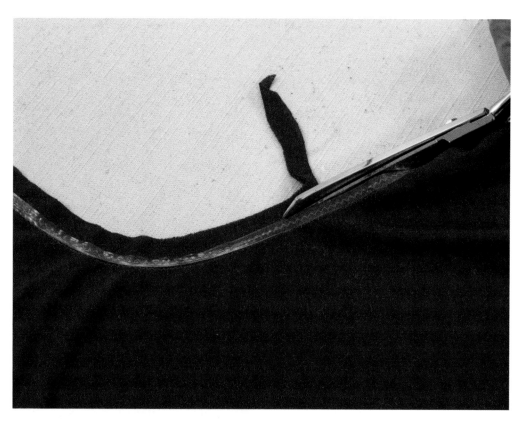

POSITIONING ELASTIC

To line up elastic along a seamline and determine where to sew, position the elastic between the two toes of the presser foot, then place the wrong side of the seam under the elastic so that the left edge of the elastic is ⅝ in. away from the cut edge of the fabric. Check to see what line you need to follow on your sewing-machine stitch plate to keep the elastic in this position. On my Bernina, if I line up the fabric edge to the ½-in. mark and have the ¼-in. elastic between the toes of the presser foot, the left edge of the elastic runs right along the ⅝-in. seamline.

2. *Using a narrow zigzag that is .5mm to 1mm wide and 2.5mm long, sew the seam next to the elastic.*
3. *Keeping the seam allowances together, sew a second row of stitching using a medium zigzag stitch or a serger, this time sewing over the elastic. When you use a zigzag*

stitch, be sure to trim away the excess seam allowance next to the second zigzag stitch.

Stabilizing soft or draped necklines that are faced or lined

Soft, unstructured necklines and cowl necklines are appropriate if your fabric has a soft drape. It is possible to add shaped facings or a lining and still maintain the drape of the fabric, but you must stabilize the neckline to maintain its shape. Be sure to stabilize the facing or lining seams using clear elastic instead of interfacing, because even the softest interfacing changes the drape of the fabric.

Keep in mind that because of the softness and weight of a knitted fabric, a simple narrow neckline facing on these drapey fabrics will flip to the outside if it is not stitched in place. That is why garments that don't have topstitching are often fully or partially lined or have a foundation. By changing small, shaped facings to what is

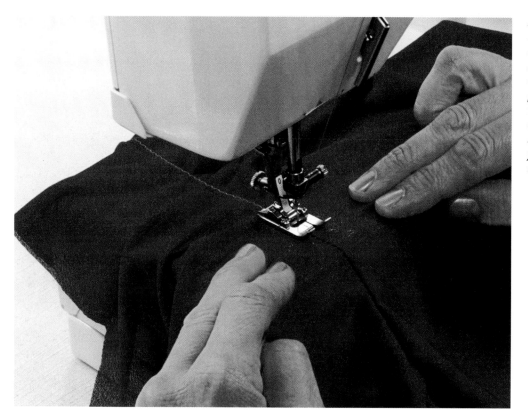

As you understitch, hold both the garment and the facing away from the seam on both sides of the presser foot. Be sure to sew through the elasticized seam allowances when you do the understitching.

really a foundation, you can counterbalance the weight of the garment.

1. *To stabilize facings, cut and sew the facings, then cut ¼-in.-wide clear elastic that is the same length as the seam you want to stabilize, in this case the neckline. On sleeveless garments, you will also need to stabilize the armscye.*
2. *Position the elastic in the seam allowance on the wrong side of the facing and next to the seamline. If you have a circular application, cut the elastic ½ in. longer than the opening, and overlap the ends as you pin the elastic in place. Place the overlap near a garment seam. To evenly distribute the fabric, divide the elastic and the neckline or opening into quarters, then match up the markings.*
3. *Use a zigzag that is 2mm to 3mm wide and long to sew the elastic in place so that the elastic can stretch without popping the stitches.*
4. *On lined garments, stabilize the lining layer by applying the elastic to the wrong side of the seams that connect the lining to the garment.*
5. *To attach the facings or lining, pin and sew the facings or lining as you normally do to the right side of the garment using a narrow zigzag stitch.*
6. *Trim the seam allowances to ¼ in., then finger-press the seam allowances and the elastic toward the facing or lining.*
7. *Starting at a shoulder seam, understitch the neckline with the right side of the facing or lining on top. As you understitch, be sure to pull both the garment and the facing or lining fabric away from the seam on both sides of the presser foot. You could also attach the facings or lining using a wide serger stitch, then understitching.*

TIP

If you are sewing a dress with a low front and back neckline, cut the elastic 2 in. shorter than the neckline size to better support the weight of the dress when you wear it.

A foundation is typically the very structured supporting bodice layer found on gowns and cocktail dresses, but this foundation is simple, comfortable, and easy to do, while serving the same purpose. Facings that are not stitched down or interfaced roll out at the neckline easily and end up showing on the outside of the garment. In place of facings, you can use a foundation when you don't want to topstitch the neckline or when you don't want to use interfacing to stabilize the neckline.

A foundation, which is easy to cut using a garment pattern, should end either at the waistline or just below the bust, like a shelf bra on swimsuits. My preference is to end the foundation below the bust, but it depends on the style of the garment. For example, if there is a waist seam, the waist may be a better place to end. Take into consideration whether the wearer finds elastic more comfortable below the bust or at the waist.

For a foundation that goes to the waistline, the waist is marked on the pattern so you will know how long to cut the foundation.

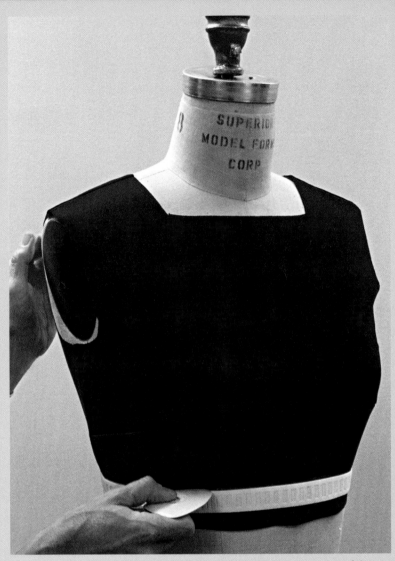

On the foundation, use a fabric marker to mark along the upper edge of the elastic for the elastic placement line. Be sure to use ¾-in.- or 1-in.-wide nonroll elastic or felt-back elastic.

1. To determine the below-the-bust cutting line, measure the distance on the body from the center of the shoulder seam, over the bust, to the elastic placement below the bust.
2. Cut the foundation 3 in. longer than this measurement so you can mark the exact elastic placement after you sew the foundation together. Mark the cutting line on the pattern front parallel to the length adjustment lines or perpendicular to the grainline.
3. To mark the back length, match the pattern side seams, and mark the front cutting line on the back pattern at the side seam only.
4. Separate the pattern pieces, then finish drawing the cutting line on the back pattern so that it is parallel to the length adjustment line.

Once the elastic is sewn in place close to the upper edge, trim the excess fabric under the elastic on the wrong side of the foundation.

the side seams from below the armscye.

8. Adjust the elastic so that it is just under the bust or at the waistline and parallel to the floor, and adjust the fabric so that it is smooth. Using a fabric marker, mark the elastic placement line on the foundation along the upper elastic edge.

9. Cut the elastic 2 in. smaller than the body measurement of the area below the bust, then overlap the ends of the elastic slightly and sew it to form a circle.

10. Next, divide the elastic and the lower edge of the foundation into fourths. Pin the elastic on top of the right side of the foundation, lining up the upper edge of the elastic to the marked placement and matching quarter marks.

11. Using a medium zigzag, sew the elastic in place close to the upper edge, stretching the elastic just enough so that it is the same length as the fabric underneath. Trim the excess fabric close to the stitching on the wrong side.

12. Attach the foundation to the garment neckline in the same way you attach the neck facing, including understitching the neckline.

13. Finally, turn the foundation to the inside of the garment, and baste the armholes together using a ½-in. seam allowance. Treat the garment and foundation as one layer to set in the sleeves or finish the armscye.

5. Next, cut the foundation out of fashion fabric as you would a facing.

6. Sew the foundation together, then stabilize the neckline with clear elastic, following the directions for stabilizing facings on pp. 146-147.

7. With the right side out, try on the foundation, pinning or tying the elastic around your rib cage on top of the foundation. The foundation should be made so that it hugs the body and is closer fitting than the garment. If the foundation is loose, taper

Resources

PATTERNS

Dos De Tejas
Karen Odam
P. O. Box 1636
Sherman, TX 75091
(800) 883-5278, (903) 893-0064

www.DosdeTejas.com

Elan
534 Sandalwood Dr.
El Cajon, CA 92021-5455
(619) 442-1167

Lingerie patterns, fabrics, and findings, kits available.

Kwik Sew
3000 Washington Ave. N.
Minneapolis, MN 55411-1699
(888) 594-5739, (612) 521-7651

www.kwiksew.com

Park Bench Pattern Co.
5181-J Baltimore Dr.
La Mesa, CA 91942
(619) 464-6092, (619) 286-6859

Patterns for free-spirited clothing.

Sewing Workshop
2010 Balboa
San Francisco, CA 94121
(800) 466-1599

www.sewingworkshop.com

Stretch & Sew
P. O. Box 25306
Tempe, AZ 85285
(800) 547-7717, (602) 966-1462

www.stretch-and-sew.com

FABRICS

Banksville Fabrics
115 New Canaan Ave.
Norwalk, CT 06850
(203) 846-1333

e-mail: banksville@juno.com

Wide range of interesting fabrics. Mail-order service.

G Street Fabrics
12240 Wilkins Ave.
Rockville, MD 20852
(800) 333-9191

www.gstreetfabrics.com

Great selection of basic and novelty knits, swimsuit fabrics, stretch lace, stretch velvets, and matte jersey. Specialty elastics and trim. Mail-order service.

Haberman's Fabrics

117 W. Fourth St.
Royal Oak, MI 48067
(248) 541-0010

Great selection of spandex-blend fabrics as well as other fine fabrics.

The Sewing Place

18476 Prospect Rd.
Saratoga, CA 95070
(800) 587-3937, (408) 252-8444

www.thesewingplace.com

Huge selection of mail-order slinky knits.

Speigelhoff's Stretch & Sew Fabrics

4901 Washington Ave.
Racine, WI 53408
(414) 632-2660

Good selection of knits and mail-order synthetic fleece.

Thrifty Needle

3233 Amber St.
Philadelphia, PA 19134
(800) 324-9927

Mail-order sweaterbodies.

NOTIONS

Clotilde

B3000
Louisiana, MO 63353-3000
(800) 772-2891

www.clotilde.com

Mail-order notions.

Nancy's Notions

P. O. Box 683
Beaver Dam, WI 53916-0683
(800) 833-0690, (920) 887-0391

www.nancysnotions.com

Mail-order notions.

Index